The Best of
MAILBOX

GRADES 4-6

D1081673

The best activities from the 2001–2006 issues of *The Mailbox*® magazine

 Games

 Classroom Displays

 Management Tips and Timesavers

 Language Arts Units

 Writing Units

 Math Units

 Science and Social Studies Units

 Seasonal Activities and Reproducibles

Topic and Skills Index on page 190!

Managing Editor: Jenny Chapman

Editorial Team: Becky S. Andrews, Diane Badden, Kimberley Bruck, Karen A. Brudnak, Kitty Campbell, Pam Crane, Lynette Dickerson, Tazmen Hansen, Marsha Heim, Lori Z. Henry, Sheila Krill, Debra Liverman, Dorothy C. McKinney, Thad H. McLaurin, Sharon Murphy, Jennifer Nunn, Mark Rainey, Hope Rodgers, Becky Saunders

www.themailbox.com

Manufactured in the United States
10 9 8 7 6 5 4 3 2 1

Table of Contents

Celebrate the Season

Celebrate the Season

Personality Spheres
Getting-acquainted project

Students will have a ball getting to know each other when they take turns sharing these completed spheres with the class!

Julia Ring Alarie, Williston, VT

Materials for each student: copy of the circle pattern on page 5, copy of the questions on page 18, 4 sheets of 9" x 12" construction paper in his favorite color, scissors, crayons, fine-tip marker, glue, length of yarn

Steps:
1. Make 20 tracings of the circle pattern on the colorful paper.
2. Cut out the tracings. Fold each cutout along the dotted lines to form a triangle with three flaps. Decorate the flaps and then number the triangles from 1 to 20.
3. Label each numbered triangle with an answer to the corresponding question.
4. Form the sphere's top by gluing the flaps of triangles 1–5 together so that their top points touch. Glue the flaps of triangles 16–20 together in the same way to form the sphere's bottom.
5. Make the sphere's middle section by gluing triangles 6–15 together (alternating the up/down direction the triangles point) to form a horizontal row.
6. Glue the sphere's top section to the middle section.
7. Glue together the sphere's bottom and middle sections, sandwiching the length of yarn between one of the pairs of flaps that will be glued together.

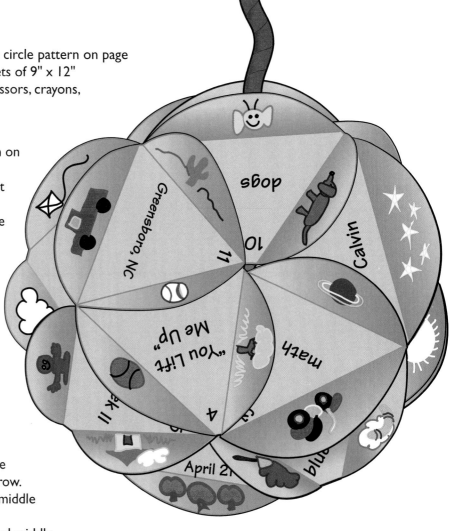

Seasonal Journal Prompts
September Topics

- A bear whose fur is sticky with honey has been stung by a bee. What could you do to make him feel better?

- Pretend that your allowance is five dollars per week. Do you think this amount is too much, too little, or about right? Explain.

- Explain what you would do if the waffle you were about to eat suddenly started talking to you.

Wouldn't you rather have cereal?

- What advice could you give a friend who is being bullied at school or in his or her neighborhood?

- Which of the following instruments would you rather be: a guitar, a piano, or a set of drums? Why?

- Jim Henson, the creator of the Muppets, was born September 24, 1936. If he were still alive, what birthday gift do you think Miss Piggy would give him? Explain.

- How are a marshmallow and a cloud alike? How are they different?

- If you saw a young child slip a pack of gum in his pocket while his parent was busy checking out at a grocery store, what would you do? Explain.

Circle Patterns
Use with "Personality Spheres" on page 4.

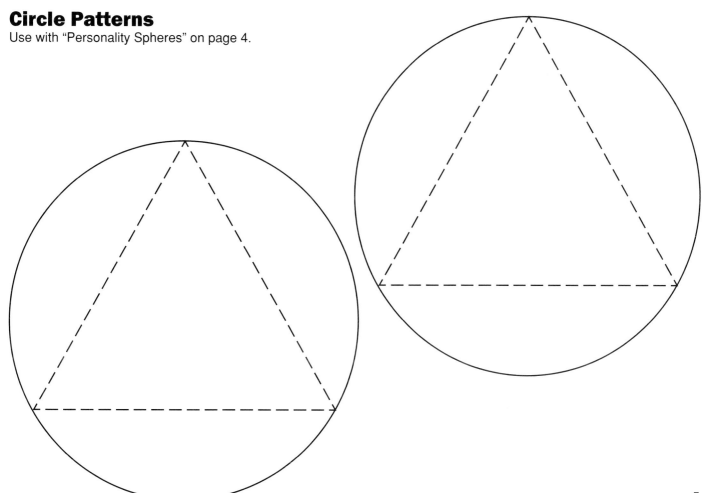

Look at All That Sugar!
Math and writing

Open students' eyes to just how much sugar is in their favorite candy bars with this fun-to-do math and writing activity. Obtain two boxes of sugar cubes. Also, ask each student to bring in the nutrition label from his favorite candy bar. Give each child crayons or markers, glue, and a 12" x 18" sheet of white drawing paper. Then have him follow these steps:

1. On the drawing paper, illustrate your own version of a funny monster.
2. Predict the grams of sugar in your candy bar. Then check your prediction against the sugar content on your candy bar's nutrition label.
3. Glue the nutrition label to your monster's hand.
4. On your drawing, divide the sugar grams listed on the nutrition label by three (the approximate number of grams in a sugar cube). Round your answer to the nearest whole number. Then glue that number of sugar cubes to your monster's belly.
5. Write a paragraph explaining what you learned and attach it to your paper.

Arrange students' papers in a display titled "Look at All That Sugar!"

Linda Hess, Green-Fields School, Woodbury, NJ

Superbly Descriptive Pumpkins
Vocabulary-building

Stretch students' vocabularies with this seasonally superb vocabulary-building activity. Ask students to bring in pumpkins of any size or shape. (Provide extras for students who forget or are unable to bring them.) Next, type a double-spaced list of adjectives, such as the one shown. Cut the words on the list apart, fold the strips in half, and place them in a trick-or-treat pail. Divide students into groups of four; then have each child choose a pumpkin and draw an adjective from the pail. Direct the student not to share her word with anyone outside her group and to look it up in a dictionary to get a clear understanding of its meaning. Then have her use acrylic paints and other art materials along with her group members' suggestions to decorate the pumpkin in a way that suggests her adjective. Conclude by having the groups take turns guessing the adjective that each pumpkin represents. Extend the activity by having students classify the adjectives into categories, such as those that describe attitudes and those that describe behaviors.

Carol Thompson, Aragon, GA

lovesick	sarcastic	awestruck	deceitful
taciturn	conceited	petrified	boorish
horrified	intellectual	glamorous	humble
boisterous	sickly	timid	amiable
sheepish	despicable	eccentric	avaricious
flamboyant	rancorous	livid	dazzling
ecstatic	gaudy	incredulous	morose

lovesick

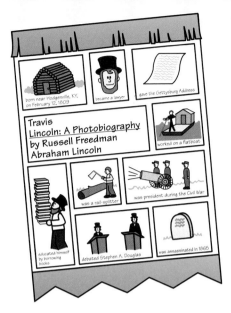

Biography Banners
Book report project

This eye-catching book report project is perfect for sharing biographies! Have each student draw ten squares and rectangles on a 12" x 18" sheet of white drawing paper. In one shape, have him write his name and the title, author, and subject of his biography. In each of the nine remaining boxes, have the student use words and pictures to provide some of the following information about his book's person: talents, accomplishments, hobbies, failures, challenges, family, life span, residence, and other interesting facts. For a finishing touch, have the student add colorful construction paper fringe to the top and bottom of the banner. Showcase the finished projects in a display titled "Beautiful Biography Banners."

Julia Alarie, Essex Middle School, Essex, VT

Perky Turkey Centerpiece
Art and writing

Make perky turkeys the center of attention on your students' Thanksgiving Day tables with this creative art and writing project!

Carla Walker, Monte Vista Elementary, La Crescenta, CA

Materials for each student: 12" x 18" sheet of construction paper, six 9" x 12" sheets of construction paper (2 sheets each of a different color), 2" x 12" strip of red construction paper, 1" square of yellow construction paper, ruler, scissors, glue, stapler, black marker

Steps:
1. Starting on the 9-inch side, accordion-fold three 9" x 12" sheets (one of each color). Staple the folds of each fan together at one end. Glue the fans together at the edges to form one large fan (the tail feather).
2. Cut one 9" x 12" sheet in half lengthwise so that it measures 4¹/₂" x 12". Glue together the short edges of one half sheet to make a cylinder (the turkey's body).
3. Cut the remaining 4¹/₂" x 12" piece in half to make two 4¹/₂" x 6" pieces. Starting on the 4¹/₂-inch side, accordion-fold and staple each piece as in Step 1 to make two small fans (feathers).
4. Cut the two remaining 9" x 12" sheets of paper in half to make four 6" x 9" pieces. Starting on the 6-inch side, accordion-fold and staple each piece as in Step 1 to make four medium-sized fans (feathers).
5. Starting at one end, roll up about five inches of the 2" x 12" red strip and glue it to the remaining portion to form the turkey's head. Tuck and glue the remaining part of the strip under the rolled portion to form the turkey's wattle.
6. Make the turkey's beak by folding the yellow square in half to make two triangles. Glue the beak to the head. Draw two eyes. Then glue the head and wattle to the body.
7. Glue the body to the center of the 12" x 18" sheet of paper. Glue the left and right edges of the tail feather to the base behind the body. Glue one edge of each of the smallest feathers to the inside edge of both sides of the body and base. Glue a medium-sized feather behind each small feather in the same way. Glue the two remaining medium-sized feathers to the base behind the tail feather.
8. Write a Thanksgiving poem on the base.

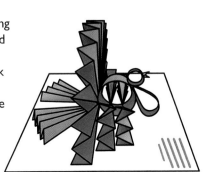

Celebrate the Season

Seasonal Journal Prompts

October Topics

- October is Computer Learning Month. What new thing would you like to learn to do with a computer? Why?

- Which event gets you more fired up: being invited to a friend's sleepover or having a sleepover at your house? Explain why.

- What annoying habit do you have that you wish you could break? What could you do to stop?

- Having fun doesn't have to cost any money. Describe five fall activities you could do with your family this weekend that would not cost any money.

- Lots of people like to read mysteries. Why do you think they're so popular?

- If Christopher Columbus were to visit the shores of the New World today, what four things do you think would surprise him most? Explain your answers.

- What type of shoes do you prefer to wear: sandals or sneakers? Why?

- How would you describe an ice-cream sundae to a martian?

- If a day were suddenly 12 hours long instead of 24, how would this affect you?

- If a scarecrow could suddenly talk, what might be the first three things it says?

- *Halloween* spelled backward is *neewollah*. What two things would create a crisis in your school if they were accidentally done backward? Explain.

- Would you rather buy a Halloween costume or make your own? Why?

November Topics

- If you were to suddenly become weightless, what would you want to do first? Why?

- How might school be different if there were no books, papers, or pencils?

- Explain what you think poet Ralph Waldo Emerson meant when he wrote, "The only way to have a friend is to be one."

- Do you think it's easier to write a report or make a speech? Explain.

- Would a turkey make a good pet? Why or why not?

- Which would you rather do: fish for an answer or a compliment? Explain.

- Suppose an aunt you don't see often visits your home and constantly calls you by your cousin's name instead of your own. Explain what you would do.

- What would you do if you started to pay for a new CD and realized you didn't have your wallet? Explain.

- What would be the advantages of going to school an hour longer each day? The disadvantages?

- "A book is a friend," according to an American proverb. Do you agree or disagree? Why?

- Describe a menu that a turkey might like to gobble up on Thanksgiving Day.

- Think of your two favorite book characters. How are they alike? Different?

Yogurt-Lid Ornaments
Measurement and art

Put students' measurement and art skills to work creating eye-catching Christmas tree decorations!

Arminda Feldkamp, Seneca Grade School, Seneca, KS

Materials for each student: old Christmas card or piece of wrapping paper, $3\frac{1}{8}$" plastic yogurt lid, scissors, glue, ruler, 10' length of crochet thread, 14" length of crochet thread, access to a hole puncher

Steps:
1. Trim away the outer edge of the plastic yogurt lid to make a three-inch circle. Then make half-centimeter cuts around the circle's outer edges.
2. Cut a $2\frac{1}{2}$-inch circle from the front of the Christmas card or the wrapping paper. Glue the cutout to the uncut part of the plastic circle.
3. Knot one end of the ten-foot length of crochet thread. Slide the knot between the edges of any cut on the plastic circle so it is on the circle's back side.
4. Wrap the thread across, down, and up between the edges of every seventh slit until there is no more string, creating a woven pattern around the illustration as shown. When finished, tuck the end of the thread under the threads on the back.
5. Punch a hole in the lid as shown.
6. Double the 14-inch length of thread and push one end through the hole in the lid. Knot the two ends together to form a loop for hanging.

"Tree-rrific" Book Reports
Book-report project

Assign students a December book-report project that decorates the classroom and puts everyone in a holiday spirit! Have each student read a holiday novel (or read one aloud to your class). When he has finished reading his book, give the student a sheet of green poster board on which you've traced a Christmas tree pattern. Have the student cut out the shape, take it home, and decorate it as creatively as possible, adding real lights, ornaments, or Christmas scents if desired. Require each tree to have five student-made ornaments, each displaying a different scene from the book, and a tree topper that includes the book's author and title. Also have the student attach a written book summary to the back of his tree. After students share their projects with the class, post the festive projects on your classroom walls. As an alternative to a Christmas tree, have students decorate poster board wreaths with cutouts that depict the book scenes.

Wendy Patterson, Pigeon Forge Middle School, Pigeon Forge, TN

Snazzy Snowmen
Art and poetry-writing

Invite friendly snowmen to invade your classroom with this cool art and poetry-writing activity!

Anita Miller, Meadows Elementary, Topeka, KS

Materials for each student: 6 squares of white paper (two 4" squares, two 6" squares, and two 8" squares), two 5" squares of black paper, 36" length of black yarn, colorful paper scraps, scissors, glue

Steps:
1. Cut two matching circles from each pair of white squares.
2. Cut two matching hats from the black squares.
3. Tie a six-inch loop at one end of the yarn.
4. Glue the snowman pieces back-to-back below the loop so that the yarn is sandwiched between the pieces. Leave a small amount of space between each body part as shown.
5. Use the paper scraps to decorate the snowman in a way that illustrates your favorite hobby, interest, sport, or book character.
6. Write a related poem on the largest body part.
7. Hang the snowman from the ceiling.

Skiing

Now I love to ski on snow-covered slopes.

Before, I was just too chicken!

But learning to do the snowplow

Has made me lots less panic-stricken!

by Annie

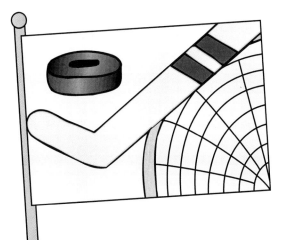

A Grand Ol' Flag
Creative-thinking

Celebrate Betsy Ross's birthday (January 1) with this creative-thinking activity. Share with students that, according to legend, Betsy Ross created our country's first stars-and-stripes flag. Explain the meaning of Old Glory's colors and design *(red for hardiness and courage; white for purity and innocence; blue for vigilance, perseverance, and justice; the stripes for the 13 original colonies; the stars for the 50 states)*. Next, have each student design on white paper a flag that represents his family, a team to which he belongs, or the class. Provide time for each student to explain the meanings of his flag's symbols and colors.

If He Were Alive Today...
Critical-thinking and research

Observe Martin Luther King Jr.'s birthday this year with an activity that develops critical-thinking and research skills. Share with students that Dr. King was a black civil rights leader who promoted nonviolent ways of achieving equal rights. Then have students consider what life would be like if Dr. King were still alive today by completing copies of page 84. Extend the activity by having student groups create timelines from 1968 to the present. On the timelines, have students include three to five events that Dr. King might have been a part of had he lived during that time period.

Seasonal Journal Prompts

December Topics

• December is National Stress-Free Family Holidays Month. Suggest five things your family could do to make this year's holidays more enjoyable and less hectic.

• December 3 is the anniversary of the world's first successful heart transplant. Do you think more people should be organ donors? Why or why not?

• The game of bingo has been around since 1929. Why do you think it's so popular?

• If you could design a new cookie cutter for the December baking season, what shape would it be and why?

• Suppose someone gave you a real gingerbread house. Describe what you might see, taste, touch, and smell in the house.

• Is it necessary to give a gift to every person who gives you a gift? Why or why not?

• What toys do you think are unsafe? Explain why you feel they are dangerous.

• If you could update the design of Santa's sleigh, what would you change? What new features would it have? Explain.

• Suppose that verses inside greeting cards could only be written in recipe form. Write the recipe you'd want inside your family's holiday card this year.

• The poinsettia is a favorite holiday plant. If there were no poinsettias, which plant would you choose to take its place during this season? Why?

January Topics

• Which New Year's resolution would you be more likely to keep: saving part of your weekly allowance or reading at least one book each month? Explain.

• Pretend that a state zoo is having a contest to name its newest polar bear cub. What name would you suggest and why?

• Which would you prefer to do with friends: sled down a snow-packed hill or ice-skate at a new rink? Why?

• Some people start feeling a bit blue during January. Why do you think that is so?

• Suppose that an ice storm caused your family to be without electricity for an entire weekend. How could you entertain a younger brother and sister during this time?

• Dr. Martin Luther King Jr. dreamed of equal rights and worked peacefully to achieve them. Why is it important for people to have dreams for the future?

• Would it be easier for you to admit a mistake to your parent or your best friend? Why?

• In what ways are playing sports and doing homework alike?

• How is laughter like good medicine?

Symmetrical Signatures
Symmetry

Welcome the Chinese New Year with a signature dragon whose body parts really stretch students' symmetry skills! Draw a large dragon's head on a sheet of poster board. Color the drawing; then cut it out and mount it on a wall. Next, give each child a 12" x 18" sheet of colorful construction paper, scissors, markers, and glue, along with colorful paper scraps, glitter, and various other art materials. Then guide students through the steps below to make the dragon's symmetrical body parts. Once the parts are finished, tape them behind the dragon's head and add a tail, legs, and a spiny back!

Richard McCoy, Laquey Middle School, Laquey, MO

Steps:
1. Fold the sheet of construction paper in half lengthwise. Trim the paper's corners to round the edges. Then unfold the paper and trace the fold line with a marker.
2. Using large letters, print your name with a pencil in the space above the traced line. Be sure the letters touch the line.
3. Print the reflection of the letters in the space below the line. Then trace the letters with a marker.
4. Decorate the spaces around and between the letters with symmetrical drawings, sprinkles of glitter, or colorful cutouts.

12

Honest Abe Bank
Art project

Getting students to eagerly research a fact about Abraham Lincoln for this nifty art project is something you can bank on! Give each child the materials listed and guide her through the steps below to make a piggy bank. Then have her research a fact about Lincoln and display it in a creative way somewhere on her bank. Now Abe's ready to be filled with coins!

Colleen Dabney, Williamsburg, VA

Materials for each student: clean, empty Pringles can with plastic lid, primer paint, paintbrush, light tan or peach paint, black acrylic paint, scissors, 6" square of black craft foam, ruler, 6" square of black felt, 3½" circle of black felt, two 25 mm wiggle eyes, craft glue, black permanent marker

Steps:
1. Set the lid aside. Paint the outside of the Pringles can with primer. Allow the paint to dry.
2. Paint the top three inches of the can with black paint to make the hat. Paint the rest of the can with light tan or peach paint. Allow the paint to dry.
3. Cut a six-inch circle from the black foam. From the center of this circle, remove a three-inch circle to make the hat's brim. Slide the brim down the can until it is just above where the two paint colors meet.
4. Cut out a beard and eyebrows from the felt square.
5. Glue the felt cutouts and wiggle-eyes to the can. Use the marker to draw a nose and mouth.
6. Cut a one-inch slit in the center of the lid. Glue the felt circle to the lid's top and outer sides. Trim the circle to fit if necessary. Then cut a slit in the felt to match the one in the lid. Attach the lid to the can.

I was the sixteenth president of the United States.

Cupid's Chocolates
$4.99 + 6% tax = ?

Cupid's Gift Store
Math

"Sale-ebrate" Valentine's Day with a math activity that could make cash registers ring! Ask parents to provide zany items related to the holiday. Attach to each item an index card that names the item in a unique way and lists a price and tax amount. Display the items around the room; then invite students to move from item to item calculating the final cost of each one to the nearest cent. The next day, announce that the items are now on sale at one-fourth off the original price. Have each child recalculate each item's cost with the discount. After checking the answers, award the items as prizes!

Dawn Murray, Freehold, NJ

Irish Blessing Box
Poetry

It won't take the luck of the Irish to inspire students to write poetry for these blessing boxes! Make a copy of a pyramid net on heavy paper for each child. Also, share several traditional Irish blessings with the class. Then have each child write a poem containing a similar blessing. Next, give each student a copy of the pyramid net, scissors, markers, a length of green ribbon or yarn, and access to a hole puncher. Instruct her to copy her edited poem on the net's base. Then have her cut out the net, decorate its triangles, and fold each triangle upward along the base to form a box. Once she punches small holes near the tops of the triangles and weaves ribbon through them to close the box's top, it's ready to fill with small treats for someone special!

Kelli Higgins, P.L. Bolin Elementary, East Peoria, IL

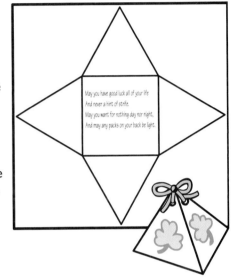

May you have good luck all of your life
And never a hint of strife.
May you want for nothing day nor night,
And may any packs on your back be light.

Easter Egg Genetics
Science

Color Code
BB = blue
bb = yellow
Bb = green

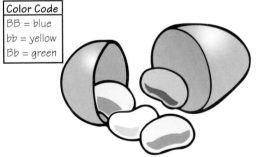

There's a sweet reward for completing this "eggs-ceptional" science activity! Make and display a poster of the color code chart shown. Also obtain jelly beans and enough colorful plastic Easter eggs for each child to have a blue, green, or yellow egg (or one whose halves are two different colors), plus an extra egg for you. Fill each egg with four candies that match the color combinations on the chart below. Then draw a 2 x 2 grid on the board and display an egg. Explain that each egg half represents the genetic input of one parent and that the candies inside the egg represent the possible offspring of those parents.

Next, follow the steps shown to demonstrate how to find the color of the egg's candies. When finished, open the egg and check its contents by the chart. Then give each child an egg and guide her through the same steps to identify the colors of her egg's candies. After students check their answers, invite them to eat the jelly beans as you collect the eggs to use again next year!

Amani Abuhabsah, Shields School, Chicago, IL

Color of Halves	Kind of Candies Inside the Egg
blue x blue	4 blue
blue x yellow	4 green
yellow x yellow	4 yellow
yellow x green	2 green, 2 yellow
blue x green	2 blue, 2 green
green x green	1 blue, 2 green, 1 yellow

	B ↓	b ↓	
B →	BB	Bb	green x green =
b →	Bb	bb	1 blue 2 green 1 yellow

Steps:
1. Draw arrows at the top and side of the grid's boxes as shown.
2. Write the letters of the color code of each egg half above and along the side of the grid as shown.
3. Fill in the grid, using the arrows as a guide. Write two letters in each box.
4. Record the possible color combinations as shown.

13

Seasonal Journal Prompts

February Topics

- Gregory Groundhog is proud of the new clothes he will wear when he comes out of his hole to predict the weather. Describe his outfit from head to toe.

- February is the shortest month of the year. If all months had only 28 days, we would need another month in our year! What would you name this month? Explain.

We almost didn't make it!

- Charles Lindbergh, the first person to fly solo across the Atlantic Ocean without stopping, was born on February 4, 1902. If his plane had been able to talk after it landed safely in Paris, France, what do you think it would have said?

- If you notice that your teacher has marked an answer on your math test right when it should have been marked wrong, what would you do? Explain.

- Valentine's Day comes in the middle of the month. Would you rather have this holiday come earlier or later in the month instead? Why or why not?

- Some people are cat lovers. Others prefer dogs. Some people do not like pets of any kind! How does your best friend feel about pets? Explain.

- Which would be easier for you to do: admit you are wrong, clean your room, do your homework, or help a grouchy neighbor clean out her garage? Why?

- February is Library Lovers' Month. What kind of books would your dad check out of the library? Your mom? Explain.

- When do you eat more snack foods: right after school, while watching TV, or before going to bed? Explain.

- If you were the main chef at the White House, what would you have on tonight's dinner menu for the president and first lady? Explain.

March Topics

- Congratulations! You are in charge of this year's kite-flying contest at a local park. Describe one type of kite that you will not allow to be in the contest because it would have an unfair advantage.

- You have just found an envelope with $50.00 in it on a bench at a shopping mall. What will you do?

- How are balloons and airplanes alike? How are they different? Explain.

- Two friends will be at your house any minute to work with you on a school project. You have just caught your little sister using fingerpaint on the poster board you bought for the project. What will you do?

- Leonard Leprechaun wants to put his gold coins in something other than a metal pot. Should he put them in a suitcase, a backpack, or a strongbox? Why?

- Describe something nice you could do for someone without that person knowing you did it.

- What are you like when you first wake up in the morning: happy, grumpy, talkative, or quiet? Explain.

- If there were a law allowing only one form of printed material to exist, which would you rather it be: newspapers, magazines, or books? Why?

- Explain what you think the following proverb means: The pen is mightier than the sword.

- Pretend that you are at a concert watching your favorite music group perform. Before doing the last song, the lead singer invites you onto the stage. Explain what happens next.

Stir-Stick Bunnies
Narrative writing

Stir up interest in narrative writing with an Easter project that students will hop right onto! Give each child the materials listed and guide him through the steps below to create a tall, white bunny. Then have the student write a brief story about one of these topics:

- a hilarious situation that happens to the bunny
- a mysterious encounter between the bunny and a chicken
- an adventure the bunny has that involves a butterfly, a dozen cracked eggs, and the police
- a day the bunny wished he'd never hopped out of bed

Provide time for each student to share his story and bunny with the class. Then display the bunnies in a prominent place until it's time for them to hop home for Easter!

Jean Juvancic, St. Louise deMarillac School, LaGrange Park, IL

Materials for each student: wooden stir stick; 2 craft sticks; white and pink tempera paint; paintbrush; half sheet of white construction paper; scissors; 2 wiggle eyes; glue; 1/2" pink pom-pom; black marker; ball of clay; various art materials such as construction paper, ribbon, buttons, and small artificial flowers

Steps:
1. Paint both sides of the stir stick and craft sticks white. When dry, paint the middle of one side of each craft stick pink. Allow the sticks to dry.
2. Stand the stir stick upright in the ball of clay. Glue the craft-stick ears to the top of the stir-stick body.
3. Glue the wiggle eyes and pom-pom nose to the stir stick as shown. Use the marker to add whiskers and a mouth.
4. Cut out two white paper arms and glue them to the back of the stir stick.
5. Add additional decorations as desired.

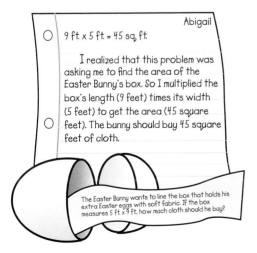

Abigail

9 ft. x 5 ft. = 45 sq. ft.

I realized that this problem was asking me to find the area of the Easter Bunny's box. So I multiplied the box's length (9 feet) times its width (5 feet) to get the area (45 square feet). The bunny should buy 45 square feet of cloth.

The Easter Bunny wants to line the box that holds his extra Easter eggs with soft fabric. If the box measures 5 ft. x 9 ft., how much cloth should he buy?

It's the Thought That Counts!
Problem solving and expository writing

For fun that combines problem solving and expository writing, give this egg-hunt idea a try! Write a word problem for each student on a different strip of paper and place it inside a plastic egg. Hide the eggs around the classroom while students are attending music, art, or another special class. When students return, announce that the Easter Bunny dropped by while they were gone and hid an egg for each child to find. After everyone has searched for and found an egg, have each student open her egg and solve the problem inside. Instruct the student to also write an explanation of how she solved the problem. Then, as each problem solver turns in her work, trade her a yummy marshmallow egg for the plastic one!

Pamela Paige Cromer, Whitmire Elementary, Whitmire, SC

Celebrate the Season

Watching Opinions Grow
Persuasive writing

Students should be allowed to sit wherever they like in the cafeteria.

Encourage a growth spurt in persuasive-writing skills with this spring display! Write statements such as the following on colorful construction paper circles.

- Students should be able to eat snacks in the classroom whenever they're hungry.
- School days should be an hour longer Monday through Thursday so that Friday can become part of the weekend.
- Teachers should never assign homework because students work so hard during the school day.

Staple each circle (in the center only) to a bulletin board titled "Watch Our Opinions Grow!" Then place glue and a stack of paper flower petals near the display. When a student has free time, invite him to choose a statement, write his opinion on a petal (including supporting reasons), and glue the petal to the back of the corresponding circle. When a statement is completely encircled by petals, add a green paper stem and leaves to it. Your flower garden will grow so quickly that weeds won't stand a chance!

Kim Minafo, Cary, NC

Railroad Math
Problem solving and map skills

On May 10, 1869, the first transcontinental rail lines were completed. Celebrate this landmark event with an activity that gets problem-solving and map skills right on track! Share with students that a golden spike was driven into the spot at Promontory, Utah, where Central Pacific's eastbound track, which began in Sacramento, California, met Union Pacific's westbound track, which started near Omaha, Nebraska. Explain that most tracks today consist of parallel 39-foot lengths of rail joined end to end. Also share that each mile of rails includes about 3,000 wooden or concrete crossties. Then have each student or group of students locate Promontory, Sacramento, and Omaha on a U.S. map. Have students use the map and its scale of miles to estimate the distance from Promontory to Sacramento (*about 500 mi. or 2,640,000 ft.*) and Promontory to Omaha (*about 850 mi. or 4,488,000 ft.*). Then challenge each child to calculate the number of rail lengths and crossties that would have been used by each of the two companies if the tracks had been built today (*Central Pacific: about 135,385 lengths of rail and 1,500,000 crossties; Union Pacific: about 230,154 lengths of rail and 2,550,000 crossties*). Explain to students that to find the number of rail lengths, they need to multiply by two to account for both sides of the rails.

Saturday · soccer practice · Kevin · I'll be home by · 5 P.M. · Mom

Mother's Day Magnets
Making a gift

This Mother's Day, have your students make unique gifts that can communicate family messages all year long! Ask students if they've ever seen the magnetic poetry kits that are popular today. If possible, display an actual kit or a picture of one from a catalog. Then direct each student to list on scrap paper his family members' names and phrases and words that he and his family members use when they leave notes for one another (see the examples). Have each student use a word-processing program to type the words and phrases in an easy-to-read font using 24-point type. Also instruct the student to leave three spaces between each line of text and to spell-check his work before printing it in black on neon paper. After you laminate the typed page, have the student glue it atop a magnetic sheet and then cut out the words and phrases. Or have the child glue portions of the laminated page atop old advertising magnets before cutting out the individual words and phrases. Provide time for each student to decorate a small paper lunch bag in which to wrap his magnetic gift for Mom.

VaReane Heese, Springfield Elementary, Omaha, NE

16

Seasonal Journal Prompts

April Topics

- April is Keep America Beautiful Month. Suppose that to reduce litter, a new law makes it illegal to use paper or plastic products. How will this affect your family?

- Invent a new synonym for *rainy*. Use it in a weather forecast.

- Write a help-wanted ad that advertises for a substitute teacher for your class.

- Think of your favorite place to visit during the spring. Describe what you see and smell there.

- In honor of National Humor Month, list ten benefits of laughter.

- Name a place that is loud and another spot that is quiet. Then explain why you would prefer to spend time in one place more than the other.

- Would you rather be a raindrop or a rainbow? Why?

- April is Mathematics Education Month. List at least five things you wouldn't be able to do today if numbers and math didn't exist.

- If you were ten feet tall, what could you do that you cannot do at your present height? What would you *not* be able to do at all?

May Topics

- On May 1, 1884, construction began on a ten-story building that became America's first skyscraper. Should there be a limit on how tall a skyscraper can be? Explain.

- May is National Moving Month. If you could move to any city or state, which place would you pick and why?

- Write a schedule for the best sleepover ever.

- If you could relive one day of your life, which day would it be and why?

- Which do you think the average mom would prefer on Mother's Day: having breakfast served to her in bed or being taken out for breakfast? Why?

- Are you more like an oak tree or an acorn? Explain.

- Pretend that vegetables are scarce and each family can buy only one kind for an entire month. Which veggie would you want your parent to buy? Which veggies would you be happy to never see in your refrigerator again?

- Suppose your best friend says she wants to buy tennis shoes just like the pair your parent bought you yesterday. What would you do or say to your pal?

- Uh-oh! You've just been invited to go to a theme park on Saturday. That's when you'd promised to weed your grandmother's flower garden. Explain what you'll do.

- Memorial Day is a holiday for honoring Americans who have lost their lives for their country. What would you say to someone who thinks it's not important to celebrate this day?

17

Personality Sphere Questions

1. When is your birthday?

2. What is your favorite color?

3. What is your favorite subject?

4. What is your favorite song?

5. What is your favorite movie?

6. What is your favorite TV show?

7. What is your favorite book?

8. How many people are in your family?

9. What is your middle name?

10. What kinds of pets do you have?

11. Where were you born?

12. Who is a person you want to be like?

13. What do you like to do in your free time?

14. What is your favorite food?

15. What is your least favorite food?

16. What is your favorite holiday?

17. What is your favorite number?

18. Where is your favorite place to visit?

19. What is your favorite season of the year?

20. What job would you like to have in the future?

Note to the teacher: Use with "Personality Spheres" on page 4.

CLASSROOM DISPLAYS

All Aboard for a Great Year!

USS BORRIES

Launch the new school year with a display that'll make students eager to come aboard! Cut from colorful bulletin board paper the different sections of a ship. Add your name to the bow with sticky letters. Then affix students' photos behind clear transparency circles and glue them behind foil-covered Os. Once you insert brads as shown, you're ready to set sail!

Sue Borries, Teutopolis Grade School, Teutopolis, IL

DISPLAYS

Watch fall trees burst into color with this beautiful parts-of-speech display! On a green and blue background, arrange a different bare tree cutout for each part of speech you wish students to review. Have each child write a word that represents one of the parts of speech on a colorful leaf cutout and attach it to the correct tree. What a "tree-rific" review!

Jessica Reis, Taconic Hills Central School, Craryville, NY

Use a "cents-ible" monthly display to keep students in the know! Enlarge and decorate copies of the piggy bank and coin patterns on page 28. Add a laminated calendar grid labeled with test dates, field trips, project due dates, etc. Each month, give each child a copy of a blank calendar to update as needed. Then watch your investment in students' accountability grow!

Andrea Wohl, Washington School, Westfield, NJ

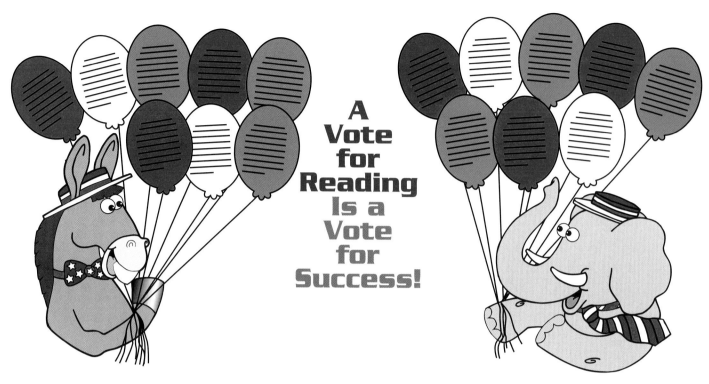

Use an election-theme wall display to promote reading for Children's Book Week in November! Enlarge and decorate the donkey and elephant patterns on page 28. Have each child write a brief summary of a favorite book on a balloon cutout and add it to the display. Near the display, place a ballot box in which each student casts his vote for the best book featured. Will it be a landslide victory?

adapted from an idea by Cyndi Smith, Fairview Elementary, Carthage, MO

Gobble up the chance to showcase students' writing talents! Surround a large turkey cutout with mounted examples of students' stories, summaries, essays, poems, paragraphs, or whatever type of writing you wish to display. Everyone will be talking turkey for sure!

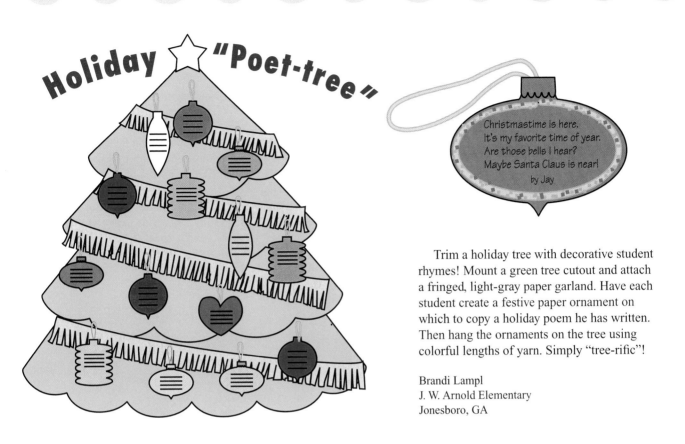

Holiday ☆ "Poet-tree"

Christmastime is here.
It's my favorite time of year.
Are those bells I hear?
Maybe Santa Claus is near!
by Jay

Trim a holiday tree with decorative student rhymes! Mount a green tree cutout and attach a fringed, light-gray paper garland. Have each student create a festive paper ornament on which to copy a holiday poem he has written. Then hang the ornaments on the tree using colorful lengths of yarn. Simply "tree-rific"!

Brandi Lampl
J. W. Arnold Elementary
Jonesboro, GA

A Winter Wonderland

Create a wonderful display that can satisfy students' curiosity! Share examples of things students might be curious about, such as why the sky is blue or how deep the ocean is. Ask each child to write on a colorful index card her own "I wonder…" statement and research the answer. Have her also create a cutout of a frosty friend and decorate it with colorful markers and paper scraps. Then post each snowman along with its matching card on a blue and white background for a crisp winter display!

Marsha Townsend, Schuylkill Valley Elementary, Leesport, PA

Celebrate Valentine's Day with a display that sharpens parts-of-speech, dictionary, and vocabulary skills. Write each listed adverb on a cutout heart. Then divide the class into pairs. Give each twosome a heart and an unlined index card. Direct the students to look up the word in the dictionary and draw on the card a picture that illustrates the word's meaning. Encourage students to use favorite fairy-tale, cartoon, or book characters in their scene. At the bottom of the card, have the students use the adverb in a sentence about the picture (for example, "Snow White smiled *affectionately* at the dwarfs"). Then post the hearts and scenes on a bulletin board.

Mary S. Gates, Huckleberry Hill School, Brookfield, CT

Adverbs	
blissfully	joyfully
affectionately	fervently
charmingly	generously
serenely	gallantly
gently	fondly
heartily	compassionately
tenderly	cordially
merrily	sympathetically

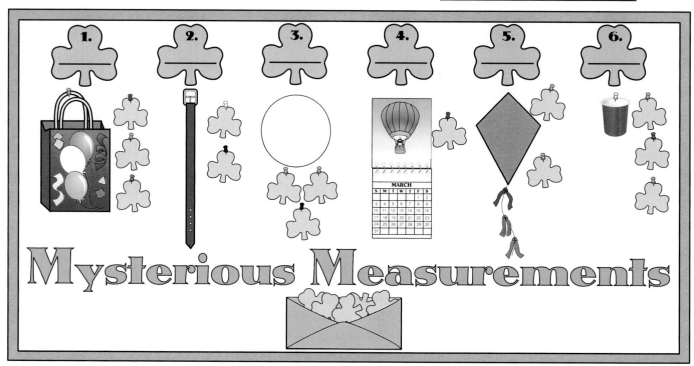

Here's a St. Patrick's Day display that really measures up! Display six everyday objects. Above each object, post a numbered shamrock (pattern on page 29) labeled with an appropriate measurement, such as circumference, height, or perimeter. Also display an envelope filled with shamrock cutouts. A student measures an object, writes his name and measurement on a shamrock, and pins the cutout facedown beside the item. Reward each student who correctly measures all six objects with a "pot of gold" (a paper cup filled with gold-wrapped candies).

Carol Buzzell, H. R. Donaghue School, Merrimac, MA

We're Big Fans of Prefixes!

For a simply "fan-tastic" way to review word skills, have each student fold a sheet of construction paper to create a fan. Have him label each panel with a prefix and at least one word that uses it (for example, *pre-* and *preview*). Then have the student decorate the fan, scallop its edges with scissors, and staple one end together before pinning it to the board. For a fun finishing touch, let students add pictures of their favorite stars to the display.

Kimberly A. Minafo, Pomona, NY

Motivate students with a display that's a real sunny delight! Make a class supply of the sun pattern on page 29 on yellow paper. Then use one of the following ideas to encourage students that they are each "sunbody" special!

- Give each student a pattern. Have him label the pattern with his name and a skill he has achieved or improved this year.
- Write each student's name on a pattern. Then write a sentence about an area in which the student excels or has shown improvement.
- Have each student write his name on a pattern. Then divide students into small groups. Direct each group's members to swap patterns and label them with specific compliments. Be sure each student labels each group member's cutout.

Kimberly A. Minafo

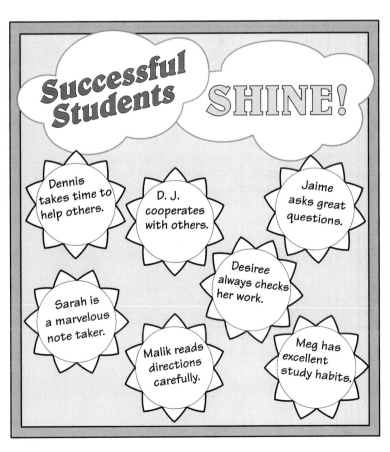

To showcase your students' math progress, display enlarged, colored copies of the frog patterns on page 30. Also make a class supply of the lily pad pattern on page 30 on green paper. Have each student finish the sentence "I am hopping on _____ " with a math concept he has mastered (for example, "I am hopping on reducing fractions"). Then, below the sentence, have him create and solve a problem that demonstrates the concept. After checking the card for accuracy, have the student glue it to a lily pad and mount it on the display.

Diana Aggas, Redcliffe Elementary, Aiken, SC

You don't need a green thumb to create this spring book-report display! Take a photo of each child reading in your classroom or on the playground. Glue each photo onto a piece of tagboard and cut it into a circle. After the student adds paper petals to her photo, have her label one petal with a favorite book's title and a second petal with its author. Display the flowers on a bulletin board as shown. For a spring book report, have each student choose a classmate's recommendation from the board and read the book. Then have her share about the book by making a flowery report as shown below.

adapted from an idea
    by Colleen Dabney
Toano Middle School
Williamsburg, VA

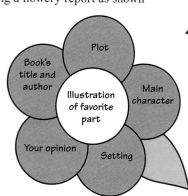

Motivate students to strive for "eggs-ellence" with this goal-setting display! After each student decorates an egg cutout, have him cut the egg in half, attach the two halves together with a brad, and staple the egg to the board to form a pocket. Then have the student insert a card labeled with a personal goal. When a child reaches his goal, let him make a paper flower to add to the display. Then have him fill out a new goal card to place in his egg.

adapted from an idea by Barb Lierman, Oakland-Craig Schools, Oakland, NE

HANDLE WITH CARE!

Use this Earth Day display to encourage everyone to lend a hand to protect our planet! Post a large globe cutout on a wall or bulletin board as shown. Have each student write a paragraph describing environment-friendly acts she can do to handle the earth with care. Then have her trace her hand on construction paper, cut out the tracing, and mount it on the display with her paragraph.

Colleen Dabney
Toano Middle School
Williamsburg, VA

Bank and Coin Patterns

Use with "Spend Your Time Wisely!" on page 21.

TEC61169

TEC61169

Donkey and Elephant Patterns

Use with "A Vote for Reading Is a Vote for Success!" on page 22.

TEC61169

TEC61169

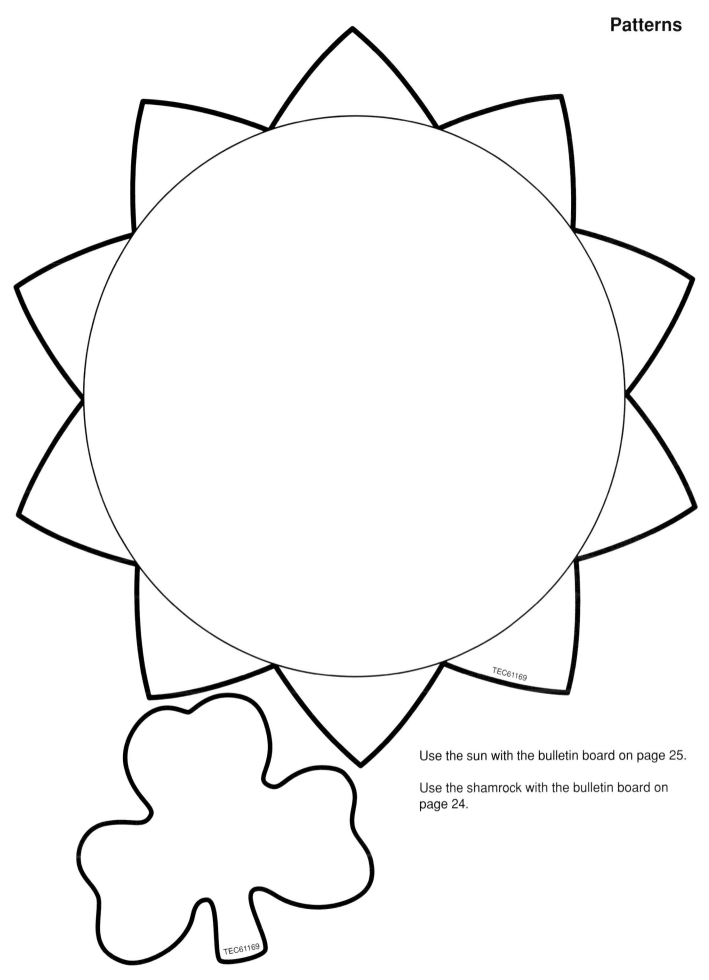

TEC61169

Use the sun with the bulletin board on page 25.

Use the shamrock with the bulletin board on page 24.

TEC61169

Patterns

Use with the bulletin board on page 26.

TEC61169

TEC61169

TEC61169

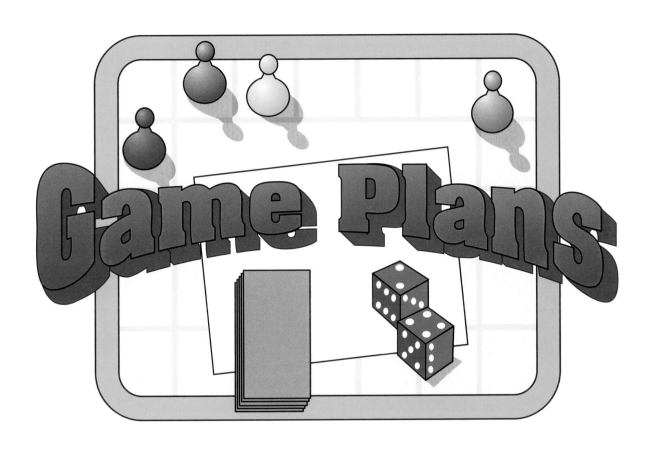

Game Plans

Game Plans

High-Scoring Hoops

Don't be surprised to see your students playing this math game at recess!

Skill: Review of basic multiplication facts

To prepare: Take your students, along with two basketballs, to an outdoor basketball court. (Or play indoors using a trash can and two Nerf® balls.)

To play:
1. Divide students into two teams. Have the teams line up side by side behind the foul line facing the basket.
2. Give the first player on each team a basketball.
3. Tell students that the first game will include the 2s multiplication table.
4. Call out "times 4" or any digit. At that signal, the first two players shoot and try to score a basket.
5. The first player to make a basket answers the math fact 2 x 4. If she is correct, her team earns points equal to that product (8). If she is incorrect, her opponent gets a chance to answer and earn points. If both players are incorrect, no points are scored.
6. Each player gives her ball to the next teammate and goes to the end of her team's line.
7. Continue play until every student has had a chance to shoot. After calling out all of the facts for the 2s table, begin another multiplication table.

—Marsha Schmus, Chambersburg, PA

Silent Outburst

Motivate students with this fun vocabulary builder when you begin a new unit of study or review skills already learned.

Skills: Introduce or review any topic of study, build vocabulary

To prepare: List ten words or concepts related to a unit you plan to study. Don't share your list with the class.

To play:
1. Divide the class into teams of four to six students each.
2. Tell students the topic. Then have each child, independently and silently, list as many words as he can think of that are related to the topic.
3. Allow about two minutes; then call time.
4. Appoint a scorekeeper for each team.
5. Read a word from your list. Tell every student who has that word on his list to raise his hand.
6. If everyone on a team has the word on his list, the team earns 3 points. And if only one student on the team has the word on his list, the team scores 5 points. If two or more (but not all) of the players have the word, the team scores 1 point.
7. Continue play with the other words on your list. When finished, discuss the words that students wrote that were not on your list or include them on your word wall.

precipitation
humidity
barometer
climate
forecast

If desired, make a copy of the games. Then cut out each idea and glue it on a 4" x 6" index card. File the cards for ready reference whenever you need a game idea.

—Lynne Kizpolski, Clara Barton School, Cherry Hill, NJ

Classroom Feud

Students will love this review game based on a popular TV game show!

Skill: Review of any skill or unit of study

To prepare: Provide each student with an index card. On the card, have the student write a question that relates to the skill or unit you've just covered and then sign his name. Collect the completed cards. Place a desk at the front of the classroom. Put a chalkboard eraser in the middle of the desktop.

To play:
1. Divide students into two teams. Invite the first player from each team to go to the desk at the front of the room. Have these players stand on opposite sides of the desk, facing each other with their hands flat on the desktop.
2. Read a question from an index card.
3. If a player thinks he knows the answer, he grabs the eraser and gives his answer. If correct, his team earns a point.
4. If the player is incorrect, his opponent then gets the opportunity to answer the question. The opponent may consult his teammates. If his answer is correct, his team earns a point.
5. If both the first player and the opposing team are incorrect, then the first player may try again—this time with his team's help. If correct, the team earns a point. If not, share the correct answer with the class.
6. Continue play until all the questions have been answered. The winning team is the one with more points.

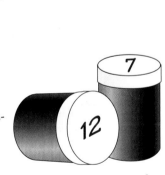

Which Confederate general surrendered to Grant at Appomattox?
Matt

—Cari Lott, Roosevelt-Lincoln Middle School, Salina, KS

The Best of The Mailbox® • Grades 4–6 • ©The Mailbox® Books • TEC61169

Can It!

Review any topic or skill with this challenging cooperative game!

Skill: Review of any skill or unit of study

To prepare: Number and then cut apart a list of review questions. Number the lids of a set of empty film canisters. Put each numbered question in its corresponding canister. Then place all the film canisters at the front of the classroom.

To play:
1. Divide students into teams and assign a recorder for each team. The recorder needs a pencil and a sheet of paper.
2. At a signal, have a student from each group get a film canister from the front of the room and take it to his group.
3. Have the recorder in each group write the number from the top of the canister and then remove the question. After the group discusses the question and reaches a consensus about an answer, the recorder writes the answer on his team's sheet.
4. The recorder returns the question to its canister and another student takes the canister back to the front of the classroom. He then picks up a different canister and takes it to his group.
5. Continue play until a team answers all the questions. Reward each team with a point for each correct answer. Award bonus points to the team that finished first.

—Barbara Bergner, Hillcrest Elementary, Delphi, IN

The Best of The Mailbox® • Grades 4–6 • ©The Mailbox® Books • TEC61169

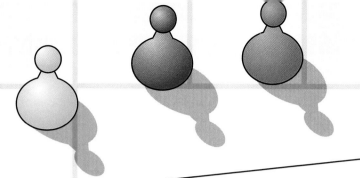

Yes-or-No Tic-Tac-Toe

Turn a familiar game into a fun anytime review!

Skill: Reviewing any skill or unit of study

To prepare: Have each student write ten review questions that can be answered yes or no. Also have the student decorate five small poster board circles with identical designs to use as markers. Pair students. Ask each pair to draw on paper a tic-tac-toe grid large enough for the markers.

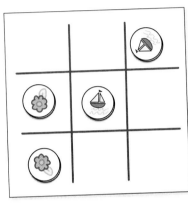

To play:
1. Player A asks Player B a review question from his list. If correct, Player B places one of his markers on any grid square. If incorrect, Player B keeps his marker. He then asks Player A a review question.
2. Play continues in this manner. The first player to place three markers in a row wins the game.

After several games, have students trade partners so they can answer a new set of questions and review even more material.

—Julia Alarie, Essex Middle School, Essex, VT

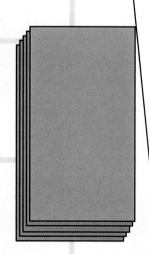

Map Attack

Conquer map skills with this nifty review game!

Skill: Locating places on a map

To prepare: Label two sets of small sticky notes with matching place names or geographic terms. Put each set of notes in a separate container. Display two large blank outline maps and divide students into two teams. Line up each team in front of a map.

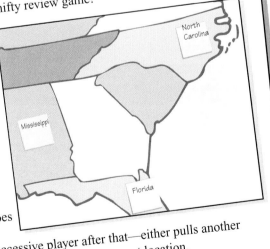

To play:
1. On "Go," the first player on each team takes a sticky note from her team's container, sticks it on the map where she thinks it belongs, and goes to the end of the line.
2. The second player on each team—and each successive player after that—either pulls another note from the container *or* moves an incorrectly placed note to its correct location.
3. Play continues in this manner until all the notes are on the map or time is up.
4. Teams earn one point for each correctly placed note. The team with more points wins.

—Juli Engel, Highlandville Elementary, Highlandville, MO

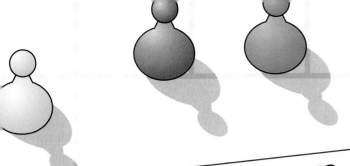

Lucky 13

Terrific computation practice is in the cards with this fun partner game!

Skill: Practicing basic operations

To prepare: Provide each pair of students with lined paper, two dice, and a deck of playing cards with face cards and jokers removed. Explain that aces equal 1.

To play:
1. Player A deals 13 cards each to his opponent and himself. Each player places all of his cards faceup on the playing surface.
2. Player B rolls one or two dice to find his target number. If he rolls two dice, the first die rolled equals the tens digit and the second equals the ones digit.
3. Player B tries to use as many of his cards as possible to create a series of basic operations that will equal his target number. (For example, if the target number is 12 and the player has a 2, 3, 4, 3, and 5 among his cards, he could record the following on his paper: 3 x 5 = 15, 15 − 4 = 11, 11 + 3 = 14, 14 − 2 = 12.
4. Player B reads aloud his string of operations. If his partner agrees that the computations are correct, Player B sets those cards aside and Player A takes his turn. If the computations are incorrect, Player A takes his turn.
5. Play continues in this manner until one player has removed all 13 of his cards.

—Michael Foster
Heartland Elementary, Overland Park, KS

3 times 5 is 15,
minus 4 equals 11,
plus 3 equals 14,
minus 2 equals 12.

Capital Matchup

Match capital cities with their states in record time!

Skill: Matching U.S. states with their capitals

To prepare: Gather 100 index cards. Assign each student one or more states until all 50 have been assigned. Have each child list each assigned state and its capital on separate cards. Collect the completed cards and sort them by region. Randomly arrange one region's cards along the chalk tray. Divide students into two teams.

To play:
1. Give the first player on Team A 20 seconds to match as many cards as she can by placing each state card to the right of its capital. Award her team one point for each correct match.
2. Give the first player on Team B 20 seconds to match any remaining cards. If all the matches have been made, remove the cards and add another region's cards to the chalk tray.
3. Continue alternating play between teams until time is up or students have matched all 50 states and capitals. Declare the team with more points the winner.

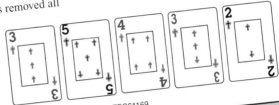

—adapted from an idea by Marsha Schmus, Chambersburg, PA

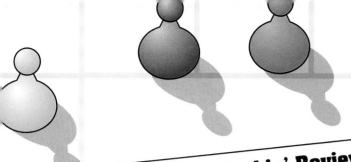

Rockin' Review

Your kids are sure to sing the praises of this rockin' review game!

Skill: Reviewing any skill or unit

To prepare: Select a popular CD to play during the review. Next, have each student write a review question and its answer for you to approve. Then have the student copy his question inside a folded strip of construction paper. Assign each child a number to write on the outside of his folded paper. Then have him place his question on the top of his desk.

To play:
1. Have each student stand behind his desk with paper and pencil in hand.
2. Explain that students will rotate around the room, stopping at every desk to read and answer a numbered question.
3. Start the music and have students move from one desk to the next, answering the questions.
4. When everyone has answered all of the questions, turn off the music and have students return to their seats.
5. Ask each child to read aloud the question and answer he wrote so students can check their answers. Declare the player with the greatest number of correct answers the winner.

—*Kelly Wade, Grand Rapids, MI*

Ask the Experts!

Let your students be the experts with this fun review game.

Skill: Reviewing any skill or unit

To prepare: Have each student write on a sheet of paper five review questions and their answers. Arrange five chairs so that they face the classroom.

To play:
1. Randomly call on five students to be the first panel of experts. Have the five sit in the chairs facing the classroom.
2. Call on one student at a time to choose a panel member and ask that expert to answer a question.
3. If the expert answers correctly, she stays on the panel. If her answer is incorrect, she trades places with the questioner. Repeat Steps 2 and 3 to continue playing.
4. Repeat Steps 2 and 3 to continue playing.
5. Play for a set amount of time or until every student has been on the panel.

—*Heather Barrett, Crestview Elementary, Simi Valley, CA*

What are three states of matter?

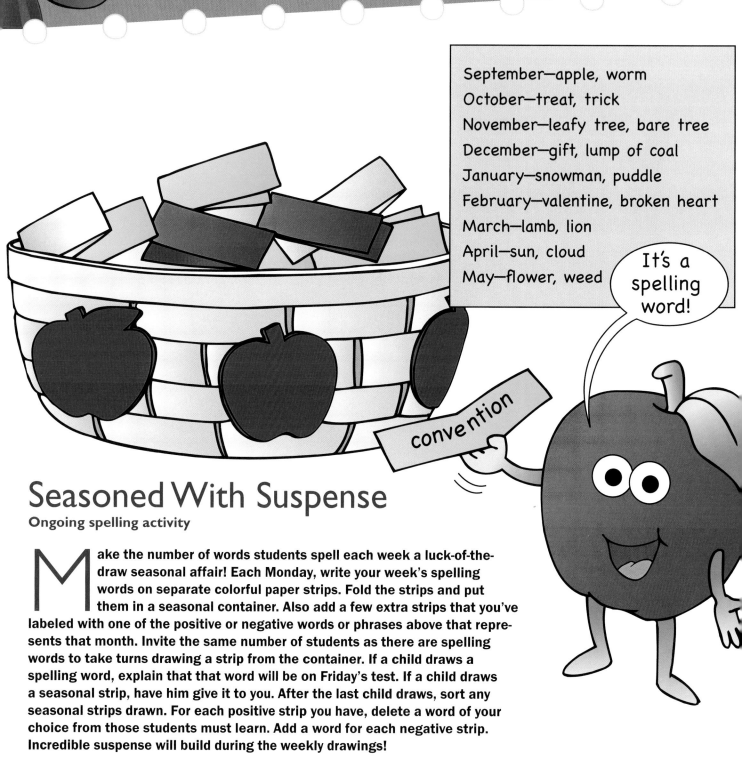

Language Arts Spotlight
SPELLING

September—apple, worm
October—treat, trick
November—leafy tree, bare tree
December—gift, lump of coal
January—snowman, puddle
February—valentine, broken heart
March—lamb, lion
April—sun, cloud
May—flower, weed

It's a spelling word!

convention

Seasoned With Suspense
Ongoing spelling activity

Make the number of words students spell each week a luck-of-the-draw seasonal affair! Each Monday, write your week's spelling words on separate colorful paper strips. Fold the strips and put them in a seasonal container. Also add a few extra strips that you've labeled with one of the positive or negative words or phrases above that represents that month. Invite the same number of students as there are spelling words to take turns drawing a strip from the container. If a child draws a spelling word, explain that that word will be on Friday's test. If a child draws a seasonal strip, have him give it to you. After the last child draws, sort any seasonal strips drawn. For each positive strip you have, delete a word of your choice from those students must learn. Add a word for each negative strip. Incredible suspense will build during the weekly drawings!

Amy Bruening and Lauren Moser, Sacred Heart School, Yankton, SD

38

Take Your Pick!
Contract

Completing weekly spelling activities is much more appealing if choices are involved! Give each child a copy of a contract that has a wide range of activities for students of every ability level, such as the one shown. Explain that students can choose any combination of activities to complete as long as the total point value is at least 50!

Lisa Laue, Round Rock, TX

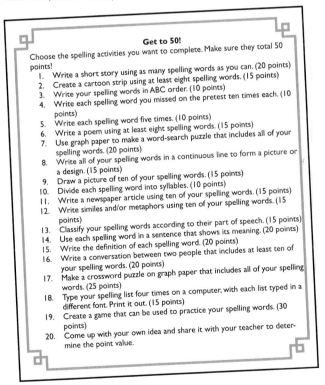

Get to 50!
Choose the spelling activities you want to complete. Make sure they total 50 points!
1. Write a short story using as many spelling words as you can. (20 points)
2. Create a cartoon strip using at least eight spelling words. (15 points)
3. Write your spelling words in ABC order. (10 points)
4. Write each spelling word you missed on the pretest ten times each. (10 points)
5. Write each spelling word five times. (10 points)
6. Write a poem using at least eight spelling words. (15 points)
7. Use graph paper to make a word-search puzzle that includes all of your spelling words. (20 points)
8. Write all of your spelling words in a continuous line to form a picture or a design. (15 points)
9. Draw a picture of ten of your spelling words. (15 points)
10. Divide each spelling word into syllables. (10 points)
11. Write a newspaper article using ten of your spelling words. (15 points)
12. Write similes and/or metaphors using ten of your spelling words. (15 points)
13. Classify your spelling words according to their part of speech. (15 points)
14. Use each spelling word in a sentence that shows its meaning. (20 points)
15. Write the definition of each spelling word. (20 points)
16. Write a conversation between two people that includes at least ten of your spelling words. (20 points)
17. Make a crossword puzzle on graph paper that includes all of your spelling words. (25 points)
18. Type your spelling list four times on a computer, with each list typed in a different font. Print it out. (15 points)
19. Create a game that can be used to practice your spelling words. (30 points)
20. Come up with your own idea and share it with your teacher to determine the point value.

The Race Is On!
Game

Spelling practice is hands-on and fast-paced with this nifty game! Give each child scissors and a grid of 30 squares. Directing her to write one letter to a square, have her list in the squares all the letters needed to spell each spelling word. After she cuts out the squares, have her scramble them on her desktop. Call out a spelling word and have students race to spell the word using their cutouts. The first child to finish stands and spells the word. Race until every word has been spelled!

Marsha Schmus, Chambersburg, PA

a	a	b	c	d
e	e	f	g	h
i	i	j	k	l
m	n	o	p	q
r	s	t	t	u
v	w	x	y	z

w	e	i	r	d

Mad Hat Recap
Review activity

In many spelling books, every sixth lesson is a review. For it, instead of a written test, have a spelling bee whose winner gets his pick of silly dollar-store hats to wear the rest of the day—and then keep! Display the hats; then start the bee with the last lesson studied and work back to the front of the book until you have a winner (use words from future lessons if necessary). The hats are instant motivators!

Mary Krause, St. Michael's School, Indianapolis, IN

I won the spelling bee!

Peer Prescriptions
Proofreading

Provide the perfect remedy for punctuation problems by making colorful copies of the prescription forms on page 48. Give each child a copy of the form and a paragraph or story written by one of his classmates. Have the student read his classmate's work and use the form to identify any punctuation mistakes and to explain how to correct them. Then have him sign and attach the form to the paper and return it to the author for corrections.

Kim Minafo, Dillard Drive Elementary, Raleigh, NC

On a Mission
End punctuation

This poster-making project has student groups putting old magazines to good use! Give each group a sheet of poster board that has been divided into three sections, each labeled with a different end punctuation mark. Instruct the groups to search magazines for sentences that have the same punctuation marks as their posters. When they find a sentence, direct them to cut it out and glue it in the corresponding poster section. Have groups share their completed posters; then end the mission by mounting the projects on a display titled "Excellent Endings!"

Heather Graley, Columbus, OH

Rhythmic Reminder
Rap

To help students remember when to use different punctuation marks, give each child a copy of the rap on page 48. Then have the class repeat one line at a time after you until everyone performs the verses with ease!

Adleyn Scott, Johnson Elementary, Columbus, GA

Say It With Pasta!
Quotation marks, commas, and apostrophes

Words of wisdom won't go unnoticed with this "noodle-y" project! Ask parents to provide macaroni pieces dyed in three different colors. Also gather books of famous quotes (or bookmark an appropriate Web site). Have each child find an appropriate quote from a historical figure that includes a comma, an apostrophe, or both, and copy it on colorful paper. Direct her to glue pasta pieces in place of the targeted punctuation marks and then trim her paper. Display the quotes where passersby won't miss them!

Amy Heuer, West Lane Elementary, Jackson, MO

"Associate yourself with men of good quality if you esteem your own reputation; for 'tis better to be alone than in bad company."

George Washington

red—quotation mark
blue—comma
green—apostrophe

Four-Box Response
Summarizing and visualizing

To assess students' understanding of self-selected text, establish this ongoing routine. At the end of the first independent reading session, have each child fold a sheet of paper in half twice so that it forms four equal sections when unfolded. In the top left box, she draws a picture about what she just read and adds a one-sentence caption. On each of the next three days, she reads and completes a different box in the same way. When she finishes the fourth box, collect her paper and assess her work. If necessary, adjust the level of her reading material. On the fifth day, have her fold a new sheet of paper and begin the cycle again. Use this method even with books you read aloud to the class!

Shannon Hattar, Lillian Larsen School, San Miguel, CA

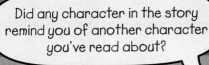

Did any character in the story remind you of another character you've read about?

Turn to page 49 for a nifty reproducible that helps readers break a long passage of text into chunks that are easier to understand!

What Do You Know?
Understanding how informational text is organized

If your grade level subscribes to an age-appropriate magazine, such as *Ranger Rick, Zoobooks,* or *National Geographic World for Kids,* use it to prepare your students for your state's reading test. Create a five-question quiz based on the text features of any issue, using questions that require the child to skim the issue for the answers. (A different teacher can create the test each week.) Take the questions from several different parts of the magazine—an article's title or first paragraph, a photograph's caption, a subheading within a different article, or a chart or graph in yet another article. Then place a copy of the magazine along with the quiz at a center and send students to it one at a time.

Angie Jackson, Flemingsburg Elementary, Flemingsburg, KY

I didn't know seals could do that!

Targeted Tosses
Identifying story elements, game

To find out how well students can identify and respond to a story's elements, place a plastic crate, pail, or tub a distance away from a strip of masking tape. Divide students into two teams. Ask Player A on Team 1 a high-level question about a specific story or book students have either read, listened to on tape, or heard as a read-aloud. If he answers correctly, award his team a point and allow him to earn a bonus point by tossing an eraser into the crate. If he answers incorrectly, give Player A on Team 2 a chance to earn the points. Continue playing in this manner until time is up. Then declare the team with more points the winner.

Angie Lancaster, Ellington Elementary, Wagoner, OK

Turn the Tables!
Review strategy

Occasionally have students prepare and ask the questions to review a story! Announce the type of questioning stem(s) you wish them to use; then model several examples. Not only will your "teachers" have to think about the story in order to create the questions, but they'll also have to understand the story well enough to verify a classmate's answer!

Kim Bostick
Kernersville Elementary
Kernersville, NC

Who was the only character who felt…?
What evidence can you find that she…?
When did they realize…?
Where was the grandmother during…?
Why was it hard for the father to…?
How could you tell that…?

Look at the title and headings.

Skim the text. Look for bold or italicized words.

Based on the clues, what do you expect the selection to be about?

Based on your reading, was your prediction correct?

Look at the pictures, graphs, or charts.

1
2
3
4
5

Give Me a Clue!

Making predictions

Before students read a selection of nonfiction text, have them make a helpful tool that'll boost their comprehension! Have each child make five tracings on white construction paper of a magnifying glass template and label each tracing as shown. Direct him to color and cut out the tracings and connect them with a brad. Model how to use the tool; then have him keep it in his desk. Remind him to use the instructional aid each time he reads informational text.

adapted from an idea by Kim Minafo, Dillard Drive Elementary, Raleigh, NC

It's in the Cards!

Determining a text's structure

This card game for three to five players helps students recognize five frameworks of expository text. Write the fictitious story titles shown (not the boldfaced structures) on 30 separate index cards. Each player is dealt four cards. The remaining cards are stacked facedown in the center of the playing area, with one card turned faceup next to them to start a discard pile. Each player, in turn, draws one card from either the stack or the discard pile, trying to match two cards whose titles suggest the same text structure. If the player makes a match, she explains why. After she sets the matching cards aside, she continues her turn until she cannot make another match. Then she discards one card from her hand and the next player takes a turn. The first player to match all of her cards wins.

Joan Groeber, Springfield, OH

Description
The Sights and Sounds of Spring
The Ideal Vacation Resort
America's Favorite Dogs
Wild Cats of Africa
Unique Insects Around the World
The Hottest New Spring Fashions

Sequence
Building a Birdhouse in Eight Easy Steps
How a Bill Becomes a Law
The Best Recipe for Peanut Butter Fudge
Learning to Crochet in One Weekend
Yoga for Kids: A Step-by-Step Guide
The Life Cycle of Locusts

Compare and Contrast
Vegetarian and Vegan: What's the Difference?
Are Hurricanes and Tornadoes the Same?
The Best House Pet: Cat or Dog?
Sizing Up Skateboards
You Choose: Private School or Public School
Taking a Close Look at Toothpastes

Cause and Effect
Why Do Certain Foods Make Us Happy?
What's Behind the Greenhouse Effect?
Four Ways Obedience Training Can Affect Your Dog
How Our Smiles Affect Other People's Moods
What Triggers a Thunderstorm?
Will Bad Breath Cause Tooth Decay?

Problem and Solution
Five Ways to Stop a Bully
How to Overcome Fear of the Dark
Can We Solve Global Warming?
Quick Tips for Solving Tough Math Problems
What Kids Can Do to Reduce Pollution
How to Help a Friend Who's Sad

Name _____

Reading informational text

Evaluate Yourself!

Use the key to rate each statement.

Key 1 = never 2 = rarely 3 = sometimes
4 = often 5 = always

1. When I read a nonfiction book, I use its table of contents, index, and glossary.

2. I skim the text, looking at titles, headings, pictures, and highlighted words.

3. I make predictions about what I will read. Later, I ask myself whether my predictions were right.

4. As I read, I form pictures in my mind about what I am reading.

5. As I read, I stop and ask myself, "Does what I am reading make sense?"

6. I take notes to help me remember what I have read.

7. When I do not understand something I am reading, I use different methods to figure it out, such as stopping and going back over the text, using context clues, or using the glossary.

8. I take time to connect what I already know to new ideas I get from my reading.

Note to the teacher: Use this page as a self-evaluation form for students to complete on their own.

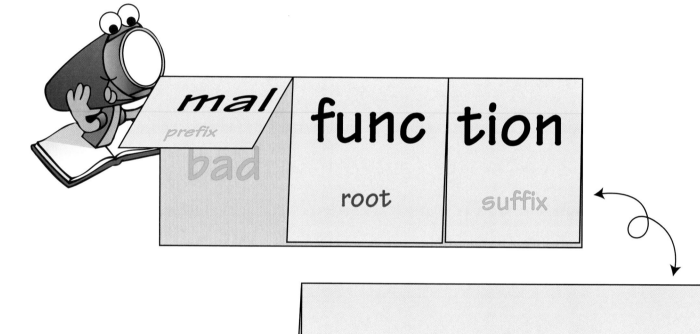

A <u>malfunction</u> of the lights caused the traffic jam.

Flip-Flap Parts
Identifying prefixes, suffixes, and roots

Learning new words is easy when they're broken into parts! Assign a vocabulary word to each student pair. Direct the partners to fold a sheet of paper lengthwise and write the assigned word near the fold as shown. Have students identify the word's parts and then make vertical cuts in the paper's top layer to separate them. Once this is done, the partners label each word part and record each part's meaning under the appropriate flap. Then they flip the paper over and write a sentence on the back that illustrates their word's meaning. When all partners are finished, they take turns sharing their findings with the class until every new word has been presented.

Terry Healy, Marlatt Elementary, Manhattan, KS

as white as meringue

as white as foamy soapsuds

as white as starlight

Sounds Similar
Rewriting similes

This fast-paced team game challenges players to make word substitutions in well-known comparative phrases! Write on the board a familiar simile, such as *as white as snow*. Give teams one minute to list as many words or phrases as possible that could replace the last word of that comparison. When time is up, each team takes a turn reading its list aloud. Have the other teams listen carefully. If they have any of those same words or phrases on their lists, they must cross them off. Once all the lists have been shared, teams get one point for each appropriate substitution remaining on their lists. The team with the most points after several rounds wins!

Patty Slagel, Ashburn Elementary, Ashburn, VA

Synonyms		
1 syllable	2 syllables	3 syllables
cold	icy	shivery
old	ancient	elderly
clothes	attire	apparel

How Far Can We Go?
Synonyms

For this simple time-filling vocabulary builder, announce a common word, such as *big*. Then ask each student, in turn, to name a synonym for the given word. If a child can't think of a word, move on to the next student. When three students in a row cannot answer, announce a new word. For a more challenging activity, draw three numbered columns on poster board as shown. Write a one-syllable word in the first column. Have students suggest a two-syllable synonym for the word for you to record in the appropriate column and then a three-syllable synonym. Each completed poster makes a great ready reference to post at your writing center!

Isobel L. Livingstone, Rahway, NJ

Keep the Boat Afloat!
Content words

Keep reading, science, and social studies vocabulary shipshape with this class review game! Program a copy of page 50 by drawing on each boat the number of answer blanks needed to spell a different content word. Next to the boat, write a brief definition of the word. Give each child a copy of the page to fill in as the game is being played. Have different students guess one letter at a time, trying to spell the word that matches that definition. For each incorrect guess (letter or word), record in the designated space the next letter that spells *sunk*. Continue in this manner until either *sunk* is spelled or the correct vocabulary word is identified. If the word is identified before *sunk* is spelled, the class earns a point. If *sunk* is spelled first, you earn the point. Whoever has more points at the end wins. The completed sheets can be used by students as study aids!

Betty Blyler, Milton Elementary, Milton, PA

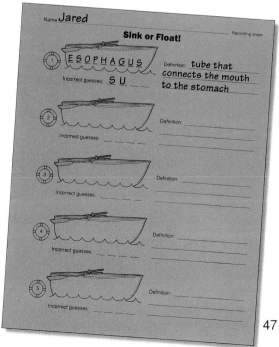

Name Jared

Sink or Float!

Recording sheet

1. ESOPHAGUS   Definition: tube that connects the mouth to the stomach
   Incorrect guesses: S U

2.   Definition:
   Incorrect guesses:

3.   Definition:
   Incorrect guesses:

4.   Definition:
   Incorrect guesses:

5.   Definition:
   Incorrect guesses:

Prescription Form

Use with "Peer Prescriptions" on page 40.

<table>
<tr>
<td>

Punctuation R_X for

Name: _____ Date: _____

Diagnosis: _____

_____

_____

_____

Remedy: _____

_____

_____

_____

_____

_____, Doctor of Punctuation

</td>
<td>

Punctuation R_X for

Name: _____ Date: _____

Diagnosis: _____

_____

_____

_____

Remedy: _____

_____

_____

_____

_____

_____, Doctor of Punctuation

</td>
</tr>
</table>

Rap

Use with "Rhythmic Reminder" on page 41.

Punctuation Rap

.
Period

When it comes to punctuation, I'm on top
'Cause I'm the one that tells you when to stop!
I'm just a dot, light as a feather,
But without me, thoughts would run together!

" "
Quotation Marks

Showing that someone is talking out loud
Is a job that makes us quite proud.
Put one pair before the quote's first word;
Use the other after the last word heard!

,
Comma

You must use me without fail.
I look like a period with a curved tail.
I'm the best, and that's all because
Without me, your words couldn't pause!

?
Question Mark

If there's something that you want to ask,
I am always up for the task.
Whether asking who, what, when, why, how, or where.
Count on me to be right there!

!
Exclamation Point

I'm tall and slim and stand on a dot.
I follow exciting words—that's my spot!
Whether you're happy, mad, or full of glee,
It's hard to show emotion without me!

,
Apostrophe

I'm different from a comma, and let me tell you why.
It prefers the ground, but I like being up high.
Showing ownership is one thing I do,
But I can also take the place of a letter or two!

Periods, commas, and all the rest—
We work together to make your writing the best!

Name

Tasty Text

Careful readers take small bites out of long passages of text so they can stop to think about what they read as they go.

Directions:

1. Label each cookie bite below with the page numbers or chapter number on which that bite of reading will focus.
2. Read the text for Bite 1.
3. Read the text for that bite again. Take notes about the important ideas and events in the text.
4. Repeat Steps 2 and 3 for Bites 2–4.

Bite 1

Bite 2

Bite 3

Bite 4

The Best of The Mailbox® • Grades 4–6 • ©The Mailbox® Books • TEC61169

Note to the teacher: Before a student completes this page independently, model how it is to be done by guiding the class in completing a copy of the page using a chapter from a class novel or science or social studies text.

Sink or Float!

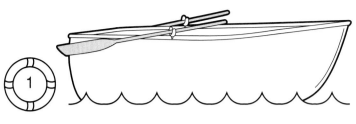

Incorrect guesses: ___ ___ ___ ___

Definition: _____

_____

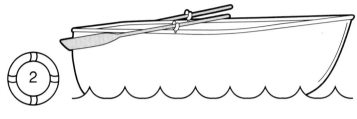

Incorrect guesses: ___ ___ ___ ___

Definition: _____

_____

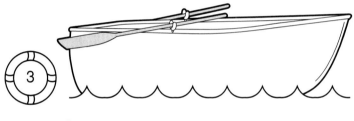

Incorrect guesses: ___ ___ ___ ___

Definition: _____

_____

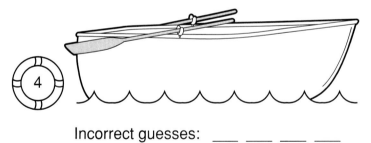

Incorrect guesses: ___ ___ ___ ___

Definition: _____

_____

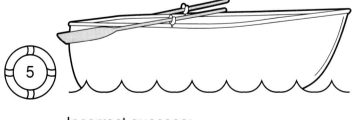

Incorrect guesses: ___ ___ ___ ___

Definition: _____

_____

Management Tips & Timesavers

Management Tips & Timesavers

Mystery Motivator

Encouraging positive classroom behavior is easy if the reward reveals a mystery picture! Draw a simple image on graph paper. Using an opaque projector, enlarge a numbered grid on a piece of bulletin board paper and laminate it. With a wipe-off marker, add any pictured lines that cannot be drawn by connecting points. Display the grid along with a sequential list of ordered pairs. Each time the class exhibits positive behavior, such as walking quietly in a line, allow a child to use a wipe-off marker to plot, connect, and cross off a certain number of points. When the picture is complete, reward the class. Then wipe off the grid and display a list for a new picture. A cool incentive that reinforces graphing skills to boot!

Suzette Pfanstiel, Walker Elementary, Florissant, MO

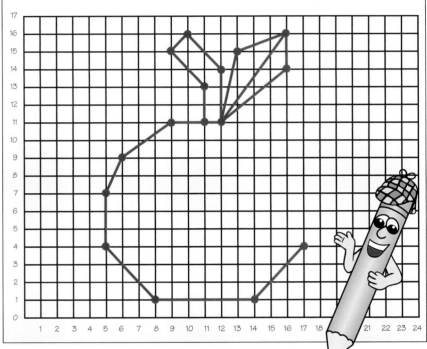

(12, 11)	(12, 11)	(11, 11)
(12, 14)	(16, 14)	(9, 11)
(10, 16)	(16, 16)	(6, 9)
(9, 15)	(13, 15)	(5, 7)
(11, 13)	(12, 11)	(5, 4)
(11, 11)	(16, 16)	(8, 1)
(12, 11)		(14, 1)
		(17, 4)
		(17, 7)
		(16, 9)
		(14, 11)
		(12, 11)

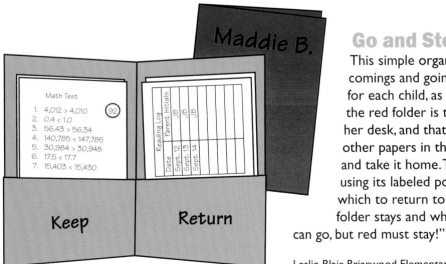

Math Test

1. 4,012 > 4,010   (92)
2. 0.4 < 1.0
3. 56.43 > 56.34
4. 140,785 < 147,785
5. 30,984 > 30,948
6. 17.5 < 17.7
7. 15,403 < 15,430

Reading Log

Date	Parent Initials
Sept. 12	JB
Sept. 13	JB
Sept. 14	JB

Maddie B.

Keep   Return

Go and Stop Folders

This simple organizational tool makes it easy to control the comings and goings of students' papers! Label two folders for each child, as shown, and laminate them. Explain that the red folder is to hold unfinished work and should stay in her desk, and that at the end of each day, she should file her other papers in the appropriate pocket of her green folder and take it home. Tell parents to look for this folder nightly, using its labeled pockets to know which papers to keep and which to return to school. To help students remember which folder stays and which one goes, teach them the saying "Green can go, but red must stay!"

Leslie Blair, Briarwood Elementary, Bowling Green, KY

Page-Protector Display

Put your class in charge of changing your student work display! Post a photo of each student on a hallway wall. Under each photo, attach a clear-plastic page protector. Label the display "Our Best Work" and have each child select an assignment to slide inside her page protector. Then, once a week, have her remove that paper and replace it with a different one. What a timesaver!

Christopher Hunger, Burbank School, Oak Lawn, IL

Lunch/Attendance Magnets

Get your attendance and lunch counts done quickly—all with the slide of a magnet! Label and tape off areas on the side of a metal file cabinet as shown. In the "Absent Today" area, attach a name magnet for each child. Make the magnets by writing each child's name on a different colorful cutout and adhering it to the sticky side of a magnetic rubber strip. Each morning as the student arrives, have him move his magnet from the top section to the one that tells his lunch preference. Simple!

Brooke Blake, Wentworth Elementary, Wentworth, NH

Once-and-Done Job Chart

Eliminate the weekly hassle of assigning student helpers with a yearlong chart that does it for you! Write the weeks in the chart's first column and the class jobs across the top as shown. Then fill in the rows by listing each child once and repeating the listing as needed until the chart is complete, making sure no name is repeated during the same week. Students will be assured of doing each job at least once during the year!

Emily Starr, Ekstrand Elementary, DeWitt, IA

Jobs Chart

Week	Line Leader	Pledge Leader	Paper Passer	Lunch Messenger	Errand Runner	Librarian	Bookshelf Straightener	Lights
1	Austin	Tanner	Brice	Maddie	Dylan	Abbey	Emily	Hunter
2	Eli	Jordan	Mitch	Billy	Ashley	Chris	Matt	Morgan
3	Josh	Justin	Mitchell	Bethany	Austin	Tanner	Brice	Maddie
4	Dylan	Abbey	Emily	Hunter	Eli	Jordan	Mitch	Billy
5	Ashley	Chris	Matt	Morgan	Josh	Justin	Mitchell	Bethany
6	Tanner	Brice	Maddie	Dylan	Abbey	Emily	Hunter	Eli
7	Jordan	Mitch	Billy	Ashley	Chris	Matt	Morgan	Josh
8	Justin	Mitchell	Bethany	Austin	Tanner	Brice	Maddie	Dylan
9	Abbey	Emily	Hunter	Eli	Jordan	Mitch	Billy	Ashley
10	Chris	Matt	Morgan	Josh	Justin	Mitchell	Bethany	Tanner
11	Brice	Maddie	Dylan	Abbey	Emily	Hunter	Eli	Jordan

Management Tips & Timesavers

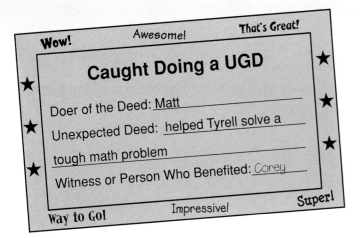

Caught Doing a UGD

Wow!   Awesome!   That's Great!

Doer of the Deed: <u>Matt</u>

Unexpected Deed: <u>helped Tyrell solve a</u>

<u>tough math problem</u>

Witness or Person Who Benefited: <u>Corey</u>

Way to Go!   Impressive!   Super!

Kindness Catchers

Here's an easy way to recognize the unexpected good deeds (UGDs) your students do for one another. Whenever a child witnesses or benefits from a random act of kindness, have him acknowledge it by filling out a form, such as the one shown, and putting it in a special container. Each Friday, read aloud the week's collection. Then randomly draw one form from the container and present a small treat to both the child who completed the form and the one who performed the good deed!

Sharon Klem, L. W. West Elementary, Endicott, NY

It's the Last One!

To make sure that original copies of papers are returned to you, mark them in a special way! Purchase a red ink pad and a small stamp representing something you love, such as a dog's pawprint. Stamp the image in the upper right corner of every original you loan to a colleague. When the borrower sees the bright red stamp, she'll know to use that paper only for copying and to return it to you. Put the stamp on the personal books you loan too!

Lin McElwee, Bear Creek Elementary, Euless, TX

Box 'em Up!

Solve each problem. To match each can to its correct box below, look at each remainder. Label an unshaded circle in the corresponding box with that can's number. The first one has been done for you.

THE MAILBOX **37**

Sticker Mixture

4 tbsp. vinegar
2 packages unflavored gelatin
½ tbsp. peppermint extract

Bring the vinegar to a boil. Add the gelatin. Stir until dissolved. Add the extract. Cool until lukewarm.

Homemade Stickers

Make your own stickers instead of buying commercial ones! How? Follow the recipe shown. Then brush the mixture on the back of magazine cutouts or any pictures you have on hand and allow them to dry. To adhere the stickers to students' work, moisten the back. If the substance in the pan begins to solidify before you're finished, just reheat it!

Susan Appleton, Grove Park Elementary Magnet School, Danville, VA

Lunch Bunch

Getting homework completed on time will become a priority if the reward is a special lunch date! At the beginning of each month, attach star cutouts—each one labeled with a different child's name—to a small display titled as shown. If a student does not turn in his homework on time, remove his cutout. At the end of a designated time period, reward each child whose star remains with a certificate recognizing his achievement. Then invite each honoree to join you in the classroom for lunch on a set day. Present each attendee with an extra treat such as a cupcake or an ice-cream bar. Once this good news spreads, no one will want to miss out!

Kris Brown, Valders Elementary, Valders, WI

Border Storage

Take your pick of two terrific ways to store bulletin board borders. Place an inexpensive wreath or towel hanger over a closet door and hook the borders' plastic sleeves over it as shown. Or put rolled-up borders inside jumbo plastic pretzel jars like those sold in a warehouse store. Either method keeps the borders organized and makes them easy to find when it's time to put up a different display!

Cami Foreman, Holy Innocents School, Neptune, NJ

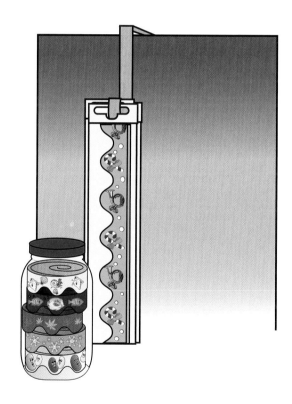

Book Sticks

This decorate-at-home project makes sure a book borrower will always return a book to its correct place. Request a class set of paint stirrers from a local home improvement or paint store. Have each child take a stirrer home, personalize the top third of both sides of it using her choice of craft materials, and return the stick to school. Whenever she takes a book from the class library, she leaves her stick in the book's place to remind her where the book goes when it's returned!

Joy Wolfe, Pine Crest Elementary, Silver Spring, MD

Super-for-the-Sub Award

Inspire students to be on their best behavior when you're absent! Simply leave a note asking your substitute to list the names of all students who are very well behaved during your absence. When you return to school, recognize each child on the list with a certificate of appreciation entitling him to some extra free time. The next time you're out, you can be sure that more students will behave!

Julia Ring Alarie, Williston, VT

Class Colors

Organizing multiple classes or blocks of students is easy if you use this tip! Assign each class a specific color. Then color-code everything related to that class—such as folders, storage crates, school supplies, and bookshelves—with that color. Whenever you find a stray folder, you can file it in a flash by noting its color!

Theresa Miller, Armstrong Middle School, Rayne, LA

Hip on Homework

Motivate students to complete their homework on time with this cool incentive! Mount and label a library card pocket for each child on a display titled "We're Hip on Homework!" In each pocket, place a card similar to the one shown. Each time a student turns in his homework on time, have your homework clerk (an assigned classroom job) hole-punch the next number on the card. When all ten numbers have been punched, reward the card's owner with a small treat!

Jean Schifferns, Llewellyn Elementary, Portland, OR

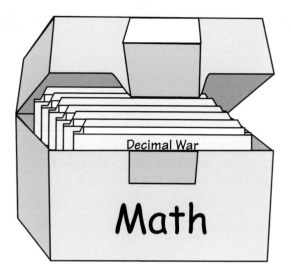

Games at a Glance

Want to organize game cards in a neat and easy-to-find way? Arrange each set of cards in a library pocket labeled with the game's name. Then store multiple sets of one or more games in a 4" x 6" index card box labeled with the corresponding name(s). When you need a particular game, just grab that box off the shelf!

Rebecca Blanchard
Harris Road Middle School
Concord, NC

Compact File Tote

Transporting computer files between your home and school computers is a breeze when you use a USB flash drive. Plus, the device is small enough to attach to a keychain!

Nancy Justice
Cleveland Elementary
Clayton, NC

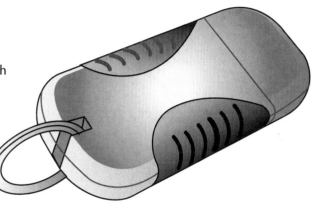

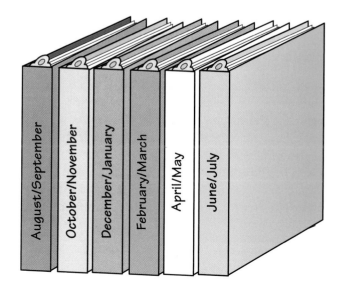

Issue Reference

Finding ideas in *The Mailbox*® magazine is a cinch with this organizational tip! When each new issue arrives, make a copy of its table of contents, place it in a clear sheet protector, and add it chronologically to a three-ring binder labeled with the corresponding two-month span. Arrange the magazines on a shelf in the same way. To locate a specific issue that has the information you need, just look in a binder!

Sharla Reiter
Southwest Middle School
Gastonia, NC

Management Tips & Timesavers

Stickers

Sticker System

This organization tip can help you find the right sticker for students' papers in a snap! Purchase an accordion folder or an inexpensive tackle box. Label each section or compartment by month, season, or topic. Then place your stickers in the matching section. Now that's an idea you can stick with!

Mary Krause, St. Michael School, Indianapolis, IN
Paulette Porter, Random Island Academy, Clarenville, Newfoundland, Canada

Information at Your Fingertips

Need help organizing files and units? Use the Web site www.themailboxcompanion.com! Each time you gather ideas for an upcoming unit, search *The Mailbox*® intermediate edition index on the Web site. Print out the information and store it in a folder along with any other ideas and reproducibles for the unit. After completing the unit with your class, mark with a star the ideas that worked especially well. When preparing to teach the unit next year, you'll know at a glance which activities you want to use *and* where to find them in *The Mailbox* magazine!

Jennifer Davis, York Elementary, Wauseon, OH

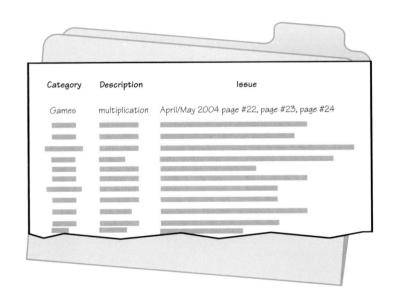

Category	Description	Issue
Games	multiplication	April/May 2004 page #22, page #23, page #24

Assignment Chart

Color your way to tracking students' assignments! Make a chart similar to the one shown, writing students' names down the grid's left side and listing each assignment and its due date across the top. As you grade an assignment, color the corresponding box beside each child's name if he turned in a paper. If he was present but did not turn in the assignment, make an X in the box. If he was absent, leave the box blank. Refer the student to the chart when he returns to get a list of the work he needs to complete. The chart is also handy during parent conferences!

Sharon Vance, Nash Intermediate School, Kaufman, TX

	Math, p. 254 (6/2)	Chapter 6 summary (6/5)						
Devon								
Shelly								
Kevin	X							
Marcus								
Andrea		X						

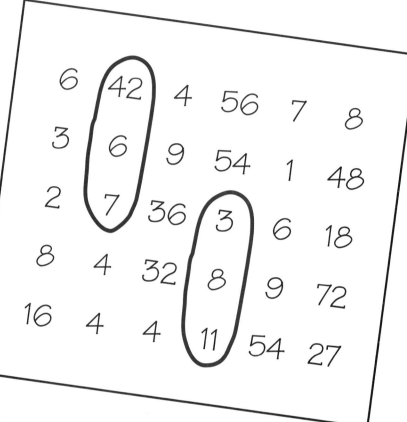

$$42 \div 6 = 7$$

$$7 \times 6 = 42$$

$$3 + 8 = 11$$

$$11 - 8 = 3$$

Ring It!
Recognizing basic facts

This number puzzle will have students running circles around math facts! Give each child a puzzle such as the one above and have him circle the facts formed when different operation symbols are added between the numbers. Explain that a fact can run backward or forward horizontally, vertically, or diagonally but that the numbers' order should not be changed. Direct the student to record on paper every math fact he finds, reminding him that for every multiplication (or addition) fact he finds, he can also write a division (or subtraction) fact. Reward the child finding the most facts with a small treat. Then challenge everyone to design a puzzle for a classmate to solve!

Ann Fisher, Toledo, OH

Art Rules!
Customary and metric measurement

Use art to disguise a lesson on measuring with rulers! Explain to students that an artist often holds a pencil at arm's length to measure an object so that everything in the picture is proportional. Have your artists use rulers instead of pencils to accomplish the same goal! Give each child drawing paper and a ruler and have him select as his subject an object in the room. From his seated position, have him hold his ruler at arm's length and measure with a squinted eye the object's height and width in customary or metric units according to your directions. Once he uses the dimensions to draw the object in the foreground, have him repeat the procedure to fill in the background. That's picturing perspective in a way that really measures up!

Karen Slattery, Marie of the Incarnation School, Bradford, ON, Canada

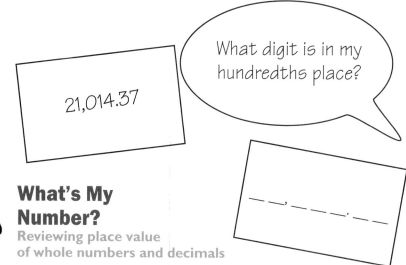

21,014.37

What digit is in my hundredths place?

What's My Number?
Reviewing place value of whole numbers and decimals

Get students out of their seats with this variation of "Who Am I?" Label a class supply of index cards with different multidigit numbers representing the place values you wish students to review. Tape a card to each student's back without letting her see the number. Direct her to draw on a separate index card the number of blanks and commas (and/or a decimal point) needed to write her card's number. Then have her walk around asking her classmates questions such as the one shown until all of her blanks are filled!

Jennifer Leon, Crenshaw Elementary, Chesterfield, VA

Dewey's Decimals
Comparing and ordering decimals

Your media center is the perfect place for this decimal activity! Seat three or four students at each library table and briefly review the Dewey decimal system with them. Next, place on each table a set of five to ten books whose call numbers match a science or social studies topic your class is currently studying, such as the 970s. Direct students to order their books the way they would appear on the shelf and then answer questions such as the following: How many books in your set round to 976.6 when rounded to the nearest tenth? What is the sum of the numbers of your first three books? Dewey would be proud!

Rebecca Blanchard, Harris Road Middle School, Concord, NC

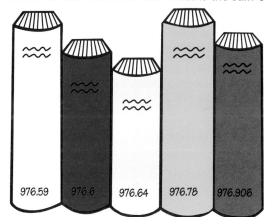

976.59 976.6 976.64 976.78 976.906

Sundae Solutions
Parts of a whole, reducing fractions

Give students the scoop on fractions with this cool activity! Provide each student with a 9" x 12" sheet of white construction paper, scissors, crayons, glue, and a pattern for a scoopful of ice cream, such as the one shown. Direct each child to cut a bowl shape and six ice-cream scoop shapes from the paper. Have him color the scoop shapes to represent his favorite ice-cream flavors. Next, instruct the student to label the front of his bowl with his name and a question such as the one shown. Have him write the answer to his question—in lowest terms—on the back of the bowl. Then have him glue the scoop shapes in place. Provide time for students to rotate around the room and answer each other's sundae questions. Yummy practice!

Sarah Bigbie, Butts Road Intermediate, Chesapeake, VA

What part of my sundae is chocolate?

Trevor

gallon

pint

Measurement Bowling
Converting units of liquid measurement

Challenge students to bowl their way to better measurement skills with this fun game! Have students bring in containers that represent different liquid capacities. Label each container accordingly: gallon, half gallon, quart, pint, or cup. Then arrange the containers as pins at one end of the classroom. To play, have one student at a time roll a playground ball at the pins, trying to knock down as many pins as possible. Then ask the bowler how many gallons (or quarts, etc.) her knocked-down pins represent. Award points for correct answers. Don't be surprised if your students want to keep playing long after it's time to stop!

Sue Hadden, Hylen Souders Elementary, Galena, OH

Symmetry City
Symmetry

Reinforce the concept of symmetry with a kid-pleasin' construction project that becomes an attention-getting display. Give each student a 9" x 12" piece of poster board, scissors, and colored pencils or markers. Explain to students that they will be making symmetrical figures for an imaginary town called Symmetry City. Have each student fold his poster board in half lengthwise and draw half of a character, plant, animal, or building on the fold as shown. Next, direct him to cut out the drawing—without cutting along the fold—and use colored pencils or markers to draw the matching half and add details. Display the completed cutouts on a tabletop with the title "Welcome to Symmetry City!"

Julie Alarie and Betsy Conlon, Essex Middle School, Essex, VT

Fact Wheels
Reviewing basic facts

Make your next review of basic facts a game students will "wheel-y" enjoy! Divide students into two teams. Direct the first student on each team to turn his back to the board as you draw two wheels. Label each hub with the same operation sign (+, –, x, or ÷) and number. Then label the inner sections with different numbers from 0 to 12. At your signal, have each of the first two players race to the board, choose a wheel, perform the indicated operation with each number between the spokes, and then write the answers in the outer sections. After one minute say, "Stop." Then give each team one point for every correct answer. When everyone has had a turn, declare the team with more points the winner.

Valerie Frey, Lakeview Baptist School, Six Lakes, MI

Candy Cane Math
Measurement, fractions, percents

Can visions of holiday candy make reviewing math skills even sweeter? You bet it "cane"! Give each child a three-inch length of string, a customary ruler, a metric ruler, a calculator, and a multi-colored candy cane. If necessary, review how to use string to find the circumference of round objects and how to change fractions to percents. Then have students use the materials to find the measurements and calculations below. Check students' answers as a class while everyone eats the candy canes!

adapted from an idea by Angela Vandevander, Wateree Elementary, Lugoff, SC

- Candy cane's length in inches and centimeters
- Width of one stripe in millimeters
- Candy cane's diameter in millimeters
- Candy cane's circumference in millimeters
- Number and colors of stripes
- Fraction and percent representing each color
- Fraction and percent representing any two-color combination

Holiday Shopping Spree
Adding and multiplying decimals

Review addition and multiplication of decimals this December by inviting students to shop till they drop! Have students bring in a variety of gift catalogs. Also review how to calculate sales tax and use the charts found on most catalog order forms to determine shipping and handling costs. Next, set a maximum limit for spending. (If desired, also restrict the number of items ordered.) Then have each child complete a form similar to the one shown for each catalog she uses. If a student exceeds her budget, allow her to estimate which items to delete and then rework her order.

Lisa Samson, Delaware Elementary, Des Moines, IA

Wish List for Catalog:

	Page	Item No.	Qty.	Description	Price (Each)	Total
1						
2						
3						
4						
5						
6						
7						
8						
9						
10						

Total
Shipping (Add $7.95 if order is less than $50.00.)
Subtotal
Sales Tax
Grand Total

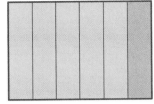
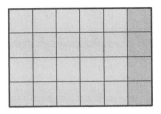

Picture It!
Using models to divide fractions

What happens when fractions are divided? Let students see for themselves with this easy-to-do activity! Give each child three 4" x 6" construction paper rectangles, a ruler, and a marker. Display a transparency of a 4" x 6" rectangle divided into six sections and colored as shown. Have each student divide and color one rectangle to match. Then read aloud the first problem shown. Tell students that their colored rectangles represent the box of chocolates. Show how to divide the rectangle into four horizontal sections, representing dividing the candy among four kids. Have each child do the same. Then ask students to tell the total number of sections (24) and how much of the box each girl will get ($\frac{5}{24}$). Follow up by having each child use her remaining rectangles to solve the other two problems shown.

Ann Hefflin, College Gardens Elementary, Olney, MD

1. Kathryn has $\frac{5}{6}$ of a box of chocolates. She wants to split it four ways with three friends. How much of the box will each girl get?

2. Andy has $\frac{3}{5}$ of a pan of brownies. He wants to share it three ways with two friends. How much of the pan will each boy get? ($\frac{3}{15}$ or $\frac{1}{5}$)

3. Aunt Helen has $\frac{2}{3}$ of her birthday cake. She wants to share it four ways with three nephews. How much cake will each person get? ($\frac{2}{12}$ or $\frac{1}{6}$)

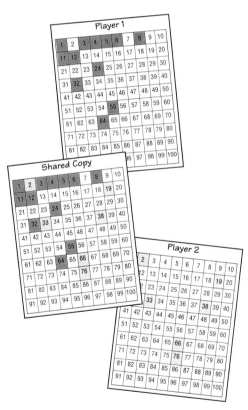

Color Me Prime or Composite
Reviewing prime and composite numbers

Here's a colorful game about prime and composite numbers that could become a favorite center activity! Display a poster listing the prime numbers from 1 to 100. Give each pair of students two different-colored wipe-off markers and three laminated copies of a hundred chart (one per player and one to share). Instruct the pair to color in 1 on its shared copy. Then guide students through the directions shown. To play again, just wipe off the charts!

Terry Healy, Eugene Field Elementary, Manhattan, KS

Directions:
1. Decide who goes first. Player 1 colors on his chart and the shared copy squares representing factors of any number.
2. Player 2 then colors on his chart and the shared copy squares representing factors of a different number. If a factor of this number is already colored, Player 2 skips it and colors squares representing the number's other factors.
3. Players continue taking turns in this manner until time is up or the shared chart is completely colored.
4. Players earn one point for every composite number colored and two points for every prime number colored. The player with more points wins.

Higher or Lower?
Comparing numbers

Fill transition time with a fast-paced game that keeps students' numeration skills sharp! Select a child to sit in a chair with his back to the board. Have another student write on the board a number between 1 and 1,000,000. Appoint a timer and have the seated child begin guessing numbers. Instruct his classmates to use thumb signals to indicate how close his guesses are to the mystery number: thumbs-up for higher, thumbs-down for lower. Those in the hot seat will quickly learn that guessing by tens, hundreds, and thousands helps them reach the number a lot faster!

Kelly Wade, Grand Rapids, MI

Three-Way Match
Identifying matching forms of decimals, fractions, and percents

Recognizing matching forms of decimals, fractions, and percents is the winning combination for this small-group game! Label 42 index cards so that each set of three cards has a different matching decimal, fraction, and percent. For example, label one set "0.25," "²⁵/₁₀₀," and "25%" and another "0.20," "⅕," and "20%." Then have a group of three or four students arrange the cards facedown. Instruct one player at a time to turn three cards faceup to see whether they all make a match. If so, he collects the cards and takes another turn. If not, he turns the cards facedown again in the same spots, and another player takes a turn. When all the matches have been made, declare the player with the most matches the winner.

Teresa Campbell, Clark-Pleasant Middle School
Whiteland, IN

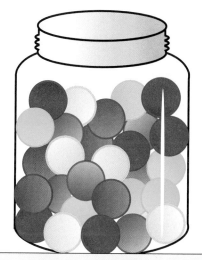

Benchmark Guesses
Using benchmark numbers to make reasonable estimates

Sweeten students' chances of estimating a number's size correctly with this guessing jar activity! Gather three different sizes of jars. Fill each jar with candy pieces such as gumballs, jelly beans, or candy corn. Make a note of the number of candies in each jar. Then display the jars. Announce that the student making the closest guess for each jar will win its contents. Next, use the steps shown to explain to students how benchmark numbers—familiar numbers such as 5, 10, 25, or 100—can help them make reasonable guesses without having to count. Then have each child use the steps to guess the number of candies in each jar and record each guess on paper. Invite the lucky winners to share their treats with the class!

How to estimate using a benchmark number:
1. Estimate how many items are in one section.
2. Estimate how many sections there are.
3. Multiply the items in one section by the number of sections.

Polygon Posters
Distinguishing between similar and congruent polygons

Find out how well students understand the difference between similar and congruent polygons by having them make nifty miniposters! Review similar and congruent figures with the class. Then give each child or pair of students a 9" x 12" sheet of construction paper, glue, markers, white and colorful paper scraps, scissors, and/or access to various scrapbooking punches of polygon shapes. Instruct the child to use the materials to design a three-section miniposter, with each section featuring two polygons glued in place to represent a different pair of figures: similar and congruent, similar but not congruent, neither similar nor congruent. The sizes and shapes the child displays will quickly demonstrate his understanding!

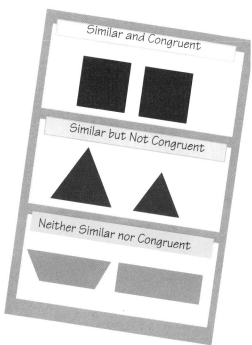

Similar and Congruent

Similar but Not Congruent

Neither Similar nor Congruent

Kelli Higgins, P. L. Bolin Elementary, East Peoria, IL

Chocolate-Lover's Sundae

One hot June afternoon, Ms. Kaplan brought in ice cream for us to make sundaes! I wanted mine to be all chocolate so I made a sundae that was $^2/_5$ rocky road, $^3/_{10}$ chocolate chip, $^1/_5$ fudge ripple, and $^1/_{10}$ cookies and cream. After eating every bite, I decided to make mine vanilla next time.

DeAndre

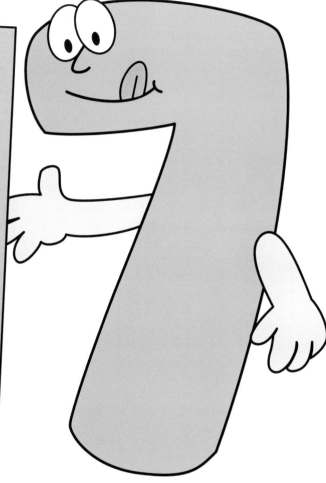

Fraction Sundaes
Parts of a whole, writing

To integrate math and writing, have students create colorful paper sundaes that look good enough to eat! Have each child cut out a dish and ten equal-size scoops of ice cream that represent four different flavors. Direct him to glue the dish and scoops on construction paper. Then have him write and attach to the paper a paragraph that tells how much of the sundae each flavor represents.

Elaine Kaplan, Laurel Plains Elementary, New City, NY

A granola bar box!

Which Box Is Which?
Spatial visualization

For a simple activity that's perfect for reviewing surface area, gather empty boxes of different sizes and shapes, such as cereal, cracker, or pasta boxes. Carefully open each box and cut along one side so the box can be flattened. Number the boxes; then tape the top of each one to the board, cardboard side out. Have student pairs number their papers and try to guess the product category of each box. After a specified period of time, flip one box at a time to reveal its type. Award a treat to the partners with the most correct answers.

Jamie Parker, Malcom Bridge Middle School, Bogart, GA

Integer War
Positive and negative numbers

Use standard decks of cards—minus the face cards—to help student pairs become more comfortable with integers. To play, one partner deals all the cards. The black cards represent positive numbers, and the red cards stand for negative numbers. Each player turns over a card simultaneously, and the player with the higher card takes both cards. As students strengthen their skills, they can turn over two cards at a time, add the cards, and then determine the greater value. In case of a tie, both players turn over an extra card and the player with the higher-numbered card takes all the cards. The partner with the most cards in the end wins. For an even greater challenge, change the operation and have students subtract the second card from the first!

Therese Nordstrom, Aldrin Elementary, Schaumburg, IL

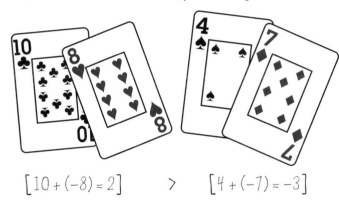

$$[10 + (-8) = 2] \qquad > \qquad [4 + (-7) = -3]$$

length x width x height = volume
12 in. x 3 in. x 8 in. = 288 in.³

Have Suitcase, Will Travel!
Volume

Reinforce your students' understanding of capacity by having them decorate luggage for summer journeys. To make a suitcase, have each child use a ruler to draw on paper a rectangular prism; then measure and label the width, height, and depth of its corresponding sides. After he calculates the figure's volume on an index card, as shown, have him personalize the baggage using original drawings or magazine cutouts that suggest his summer plans. For more practice, collect the index cards and display the suitcases. Then challenge the class to match the cards to the corresponding bags!

Melissa Bryan, Valley Forge Middle School, Wayne, PA

Vacation on the Go!

Plan a family trip to two theme parks. Spend less than $400. Include a two-night hotel stay and two meals per day.

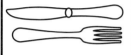

Family Meal Deals

(Meal Deals include drinks and side items.)

- **Pizza Dinner** $26.80
- **Hamburgers** $22.50
- **Steak Feast** $57.60

Weekend Getaway

Day One

Park: _____ Cost: $_____

Lunch: _____ Cost: $_____

Dinner: _____ Cost: $_____

Hotel: _____ Cost: $_____

Day Two

Park: _____ Cost: $_____

Lunch: _____ Cost: $_____

Dinner: _____ Cost: $_____

Hotel: _____ Cost: $_____

Total Cost: $_____

Hotels

CITY HOTEL $60.00 per night

- indoor pool and exercise room
- free breakfast

Hidden Marvel Resort and Hotel $100 per night

- ○ all the comforts of home
- ○ indoor pool and game room
- ○ free breakfast

Theme Parks

Imagination Way Family Admission Price $85.00

Imagination Way — Visit during Alien Week!

Sea Creature Water Park $52.50 Family Ticket Price

Sea Creature Water Park — 38 Wet 'n' Wacky Rides

SPORTS CITY CENTRAL — All-Sports Theme Park

Sports City Central All-Day Family Pass $96.95

Watch 'em Grow!

Friendly bookworms grow longer throughout the year with these colorful reading records! I have each child make a face for her bookworm by tracing a large roll of masking tape on colorful construction paper and decorating the cutout with wiggle eyes, markers, and other craft materials. Once she writes her name on the face, I display it at the top of a bulletin board titled "We Are Bookworms!" My students cut out additional circles and place them in a basket near the board. Each time a child reads a book, I have her write the book title and author on a blank circle and add it to her record. By the end of the year, she has quite a long worm to take home!

Brooke Blake, Wentworth Elementary, Wentworth, NH

Test-Day Sentences

Leave the writing of sentences for spelling tests to your class! Each time my students write sentences with their spelling or vocabulary words, I have each child draw a smiley face next to the sentence he thinks is the best. When I give the spelling or vocabulary test, I use my students' sentences to illustrate the words. They love hearing me read what they wrote!

Isobel L. Livingstone
Rahway, NJ

○	1. That cat is timid.
	2. Dad hopes a new catalog comes in the mail today.
☺	3. I cringe each time I hear that shrill, eerie noise.
	4. Will we visit the zoo tomorrow?
	5. The telephone kept ringing.
○	

Sound-Inspired Stories

Give first-day-of-school writing assignments a cool twist! I play a CD or cassette tape of soothing sounds, such as a gurgling brook or chirping birds. Without identifying the sound, I ask each child to write a creative story that incorporates the sounds. My students are surprised because they expect the usual topic— "What I Did on My Summer Vacation!"

Jennifer Jack
Harding School
Kenilworth, NJ

Chirp, chirp!

Gurgle, gurgle!

Lend a Hand!

Communicate to parents any school supplies and classroom assistance anticipated during the year with this handy idea! On a board titled "Lend a Hand!" I display colorful hand cutouts, each labeled with a different item or task. I point out the display to parents and family members when they come to school for open house or conferences. Before I know it, my needs and requests have all been met!

printer paper

disposable cameras

Julian Gale, Oakland Elementary, Greenwood, SC

Calendar Reminders

Students' birthdays won't be overlooked if they're posted on a large calendar! Each child writes his name and birthdate on the back of a small birthday cake cutout, and then he decorates the front. I collect the decorated cutouts and use a permanent marker to write each child's name and birthdate on the decorated side. At the first of each month, I post the appropriate cutouts on my classroom calendar. To recognize an approaching birthday, I say something such as, "Today is September 12. How many days are there until Jeff's birthday?" That child smiles as his classmates check the calendar to find the answer!

Michelle Bauml, Houston ISD, Houston, TX

Two-Color Editing

Pencils with blue lead at one end and red at the other are perfect tools for peer editing! When my students edit their own papers, I have them use the pencil's red end. When they edit each other's work, I have them use the blue end!

Phyllis Bieri, North Middle School, Saginaw, MI

Cinco

Morning work is a breeze with this easy-to-use form! On Mondays, we write five tasks on the board—a sentence full of errors to correct, a math problem to solve, and questions that review other subject areas. We also give each child a copy of a form on which to record her answers. The form has five sections, and each section has boxes for five answers plus the day's date. If we copy the form front and back, it becomes a ten-day form!

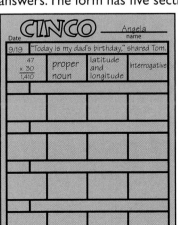

Carol Gerber and Linda Smith
Ossian Elementary
Ossian, IN

Explorer Trading Cards

Capitalize on the sports card craze to help students remember explorers or other important people they will study. For each explorer we study, I give each child half of a 3" x 5" unlined index card. On one side, I direct him to name and illustrate that explorer. On the other side, I have the child list the information shown. We store the completed cards at a center in clear plastic sleeves like those used by serious card collectors!

Dawn Matthews
Roxboro Road Elementary
Syracuse, NY

Explorer: Henry Hudson
Countries Sailed For: England, Holland
Year(s) of Exploration: 1607–1611
Place(s) Explored: Chesapeake Bay, Delaware Bay, Hudson River, Hudson Bay, Hudson Strait

Memorable Anecdotes

Announce your student of the week using a personal anecdote! The first day of school, I send home an index card with a note asking parents or guardians to describe on the card a memorable time that their child would not mind being shared with the class. I request that the anecdote not name the child and that it begin "I remember the time my child." Each time I announce a new student of the week, I have the honoree stand as I read his personal anecdote. Afterward, I ask his classmates to write positive thoughts on separate index cards that I collect and hole punch. Then I tie the collected cards together with the parent's card on top. During the week, I share several more cards aloud. At the end of the week, I send the rest home with the child as a special memento!

Kim Minafo
Dillard Drive Elementary
Raleigh, NC

I remember the time my child brought home a handprint he'd made in school. I use that gift as a paperweight on my desk at work. Each time I look at the craft, it reminds me how much I love him!

It's in the Bag!

Use this creative timeline to help students remember important events and dates in history. Gather duct tape, 8½" x 11" white paper, and a supply of gallon-size plastic resealable bags. Tape the bags, as shown, and display them on a bulletin board or wall. After a history lesson, choose a student to illustrate the lesson's most important event on white paper, labeling the paper with the event's name and date. Then slip the illustration into the next plastic bag in line. With this versatile timeline, remembering important events and dates will be in the bag!

Michelle Holstein
East Hardy Early Middle School, Baker, WV

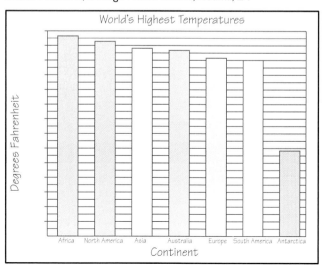

Dynamic Data Graphs

Give your class real-life graphing practice by having students graph interesting data from an almanac. Make enough copies of almanac pages so that each child has a wide selection of intriguing data to choose from. Then have each student create a graph that best represents his chosen data. Hang the graphs on a display titled "Dynamic Data."

Brandi Holcomb, Dularge Middle School, Houma, LA

Good-Manners Mints

Encourage the use of good manners with this simple idea. Fill a jar with peppermints and place it in your classroom. Announce that each student may request one mint per day. Then explain that a student will be given a mint only if she uses good manners and says, "May I," "Please," and "Thank you." What an easy way to mint good manners throughout the day!

Teresa Page, Mid Rivers Elementary, St. Peters, MO

A Year in Photos

Promote parent communication with this picture-perfect idea! Ask each child's parents to send in a disposable camera. Throughout the year, take pictures of the student participating in a variety of tasks. When his camera is filled, send it home for developing and encourage the parent to send another. What an easy way to give busy parents a picture of their child's school day!

Kathleen Jones, Anna Jarvis Elementary, Grafton, WV

Pop-the-Top Day

If Halloween celebrations are off-limits at your school, try a fun Halloween alternative that focuses on reading. Designate the school day closest to Halloween as Pop-the-Top Day. Two weeks in advance, have each student choose a book to read. Explain that on the special day each child will dress as a character from her book and present a book report. Give students time to read their books, complete their reports, and plan their costumes. Also invite parents to attend the celebration. Then, on the appointed day, have each child present her report. Afterward, have each student read a favorite part of her book to a partner and then pop the top on a can of soda to celebrate a job well done!

Jennifer Nelson, Jacksonville, FL

New Unit Postcards

Are your students getting ready to explore the 50 states, dive into the ocean, or blast off into space? At the start of each new unit or theme, have each child write a postcard to his parents describing the learning adventure that's ahead. Mail the postcards a week before you begin the unit. Not only will interest in the new topic increase, but students will also get the chance to practice their real-world writing skills. Plus it's an easy way to keep parents informed of classroom happenings.

Anastasia Epstein, North Barrington School, Barrington, IL

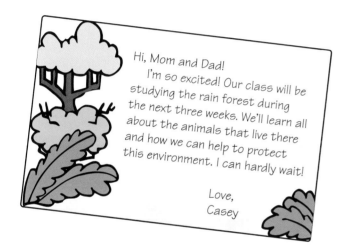

Hi, Mom and Dad!
I'm so excited! Our class will be studying the rain forest during the next three weeks. We'll learn all about the animals that live there and how we can help to protect this environment. I can hardly wait!

Love,
Casey

Author's Corner

Make writing the activity of choice in your classroom with this idea! Check out yard sales or your school's basement for a discarded desk and chair that need just a little TLC. (If desired, decoupage the furniture with pages, words, and quotes cut from discarded books and magazines.) Then place the furniture in a corner of your room to create a special Author's Corner. Stock the area with items such as the following:
- a basket filled with Newbery Medal–winning books, a thesaurus, and a dictionary
- a container of fun writing tools, such as a feather pen, a giant pencil, or gel pens
- several acrylic frames to hold samples of students' written work
- copies of class books and anthologies

Each Monday choose one child to sit at the desk through Friday to serve as Author of the Week. It's the "write" way to make writing a class favorite!

Kerri Drabek, Toledo, OH

Reminder Rings

Tired of writing notes to remind forgetful students about returning signed report cards or bringing in field trip money? Here's a simple solution to the "I forgot" syndrome. Collect a supply of the small plastic safety seals found on orange juice cartons with screw-on tops. Then have a forgetful student slip a seal on his finger before he heads home. What a handy reminder!

Colleen Dabney, Toano Middle School, Williamsburg, VA

Find Three!

Lend a hand to your second-language students with a guessing game that sharpens everyone's thinking skills. Write each category shown below on a separate index card. Then divide the class into groups. Secretly give one card to each group with directions to locate three classroom objects that fit the category. Have students write each object's name on a separate sticky note. When students are finished, ask each group, in turn, to read its three notes and affix them to the objects without identifying the category. Then challenge the class to think about the objects' shared attributes and guess the category. To assist your second-language students, leave the notes on the items. Repeat the activity as you cover new concepts throughout the year.

Fran Rotole
Goldrick Elementary
Denver, CO

- mobile objects
- wooden objects
- plastic objects
- electric objects
- audible objects
- transparent objects
- objects more expensive than $10
- objects less expensive than $10
- objects lighter than your math book
- objects heavier than your math book

CD player

tape player

Dry-Erase Board Eraser

My students love to use dry-erase boards, but I needed an eraser alternative. The answer to my problem was foam paintbrushes. They are inexpensive, reusable, and easy to clean. My students keep the brushes in their desks until they need them, and when they are done, they rinse them with water to clean them.

Shelia Walker,
Reedy Creek Elementary,
Charlotte, NC

Showered With Kindness

I cultivate character development with this neat idea. First, I hang an umbrella upside down in my classroom. I also label a supply of paper slips with the text shown. I invite a child to fill out a slip each time she sees a classmate showing kindness. Then I have her fold the slip and place it in the umbrella. At the end of each week, I select a few strips to share with the class. Then I reward each recognized student with a small treat.

Dana Bruegenhemke, Forest Park Elementary, O'Fallon, MO

Kid-Created Window Clings

Brighten up your classroom with homemade window clings! I buy clear ten-gauge plastic at a local fabric store and cut it into squares. Next, I photocopy several different simple pieces of seasonal clip art. I place the copies at a center along with the plastic squares and permanent markers. Then I have each student choose one piece of clip art, cover it with a plastic square, and use the markers to trace and color the shape onto the plastic. When he is finished, I have him place the plastic on the inside of a classroom window, where it sticks on its own throughout the season. The kids love it!

Joyce Hovanec, Glassport Elementary, Glassport, PA

Calling All Readers!

Make read-aloud time less noisy with a class set of reading phones! To make each handset, I use one four-inch length of half-inch PVC pipe (most home improvement stores will cut the pipe for you) and two 90-degree elbows. After I attach an elbow to each end of the pipe, as shown, the handset is ready to use. When the student holds the phone up to his ear, he can read aloud to himself without distracting anyone else around him. Now quieter read-aloud time is just a phone call away!

Jill Reeves, Krisle Elementary
Springfield, TN

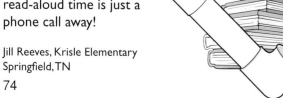

Terminator Table

Turn the tables on ordinary review games with this fast-paced challenge! I place a call bell in the middle of a tabletop at the front of the room. Then I have two students stand on either side of the table, each with one hand flat on the tabletop and one hand behind his back. I ask a review question. The first player to ring the bell has five seconds to answer the question. If correct, he stays for another question, and his opponent is terminated. If incorrect, his opponent gets a chance to answer correctly and terminate him. If neither player is correct, they are both eliminated and replaced by new players. Play continues in this manner with each new question asked. The winner is the student who terminates the most players.

Patricia Rigueira, Southern Cross School, Beccar, Buenos Aires, Argentina

End-of-the-Year Photo Posters

For an end-of-the-year gift that students will dub picture-perfect, try this idea! A few weeks before the school year's end, ask a colleague to take a photo of you and your class. Order copies of the picture (one per student). Then glue each photo onto a large piece of oaktag. On the last day of school, set out a collection of fun writing utensils and give each child one of the posters. Then invite students to use the writing tools for autographing each other's posters.

Patty Boniti, St. Joseph the Worker School, Weirton, WV

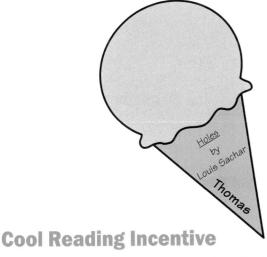

Cool Reading Incentive

Make reading a hot topic with a cool reading incentive! Title a bulletin board "Reading Is Cool!" Each time a student finishes a reading-level-appropriate book, have him label a brown paper ice cream cone with his name and the book's title and author. Then have him color a white ice cream scoop pattern, glue it to the cone, and pin the cutout on the board. When the 100th cone is added to the display, celebrate your class's reading accomplishments with an ice cream party. How cool!

Ami Hannawald, Butler Elementary, Butler, OH

Mental Moments

Grab a bag of M&M's candies for a quick and tasty review! Write each student's name on a separate slip of paper. Then place the slips in a paper bag. Periodically announce, "It's time for a Mental Moment!" Then draw a name and ask that child a review question. If the student answers correctly, have her roll a die. Then reward her with that number of M&M's candies. If desired, post a colorful M&M's candy cutout on your chalkboard to alert students that a Mental Moment is moments away!

Linda Cummer, Gibraltar School, Fish Creek, WI

Summer Reading Recommendations

Send students home this summer with a reading list that reminds them of the past year! First, list class read-alouds and other books student groups have read this year. Locate the entry for each book on an online bookstore's Web site, such as Amazon.com. Click on a link that gives related titles, such as "Customers who bought this book also bought…" or "Explore similar items." Then record at least two related titles and their authors for each book on your list. Use the information to create a summer reading list as shown. Give each student a copy of the reading recommendations at the end of the year.

Leslie Russell, M. L. King School, Piscataway, NJ

Summer Reading Recommendations

If you enjoyed reading *Gathering Blue* by Lois Lowry, try the following books:
- *The Giver* by Lois Lowry
- *Summerland* by Michael Chabon

If you enjoyed reading *Just Juice* by Karen Hesse, try the following books:
- *Love That Dog* by Sharon Creech
- *Molly's Pilgrim* by Barbara Cohen

End-of-the-Year Bookmarks

Mark the end of a great year by giving each of your students a forget-me-not bookmark! Ask a colleague to take a photo of you with each child. After the photos are developed, follow these steps to make each student's bookmark:

1. Trim the photo so it is the size of a small bookmark as shown.
2. Use a word-processing program to type a poem such as the one shown or other words of wisdom. Reduce the font size and adjust the margins so that the message will fit on the back of the bookmark. Print one copy.
3. Cut out the message and glue it to the back of the bookmark. Laminate the bookmark.
4. Punch a hole in the top of the bookmark. Loop a length of colored ribbon or yarn through the hole.

Joseph Lemmo, Chapman Intermediate School, Woodstock, GA

Go out into the world.
Be brilliant; be kind.
Always remember that
You were a student of mine!

Never forget your fifth-grade year and the teacher who cared about you so much.

Sincerely,
Mr. Lemmo

2003

"Tech" It Out!

Searching for an easy way to tie technology to your current units of study? Divide students into small groups. Assign to each group a Web site that is related to a topic students are currently studying. Direct the group to "tech out" its site and list ten questions that can be answered using the information on it. Place each group's questions (along with an answer key) in a folder near your classroom computer. Then, when a student has free time, have him choose a set of questions to answer.

Marsha Schmus—Chambersburg, PA

Displaying Paperbacks

Do you often display new books in your classroom? To display paperback books that don't stand up easily, use plastic plate stands. They do the same job as expensive book holders at a much lower cost!

Miguelina Ortiz, Steele School, Baldwin, NY

Summer Planning Day

A few weeks before the new school year begins, all five teachers on our grade level meet at my house for an all-day planning session. Each teacher brings her plan book, teacher's guides, and a potluck dish for lunch. While we plan the year ahead, each of us labels a blank calendar with upcoming units, projects, field trips, testing dates, and other special events. When we're finished, everyone has a master calendar for the year. It's a long day, but it pays off in making the year run smoothly.

Joan Mosley, Curtis Creek Elementary, Sonora, CA

SEASONAL & HOLIDAY REPROS

Triple (and Quadruple) Trouble!

Mr. Jones knows he's in for a challenging year. He's just been given the names of the boys and girls who are in his upcoming class. The problem? He's discovered he will have not one, not two, but *three* sets of triplets! In addition, he'll have a set of quadruplets in his class!

Help Mr. Jones combine all of the boys' and girls' names below into a class roster. List all of the students' names in alphabetical order on the blanks provided, last names first. Check off each name as you write it. The list has been started for you.

boys

Paul Hawkes

Austin Whitted

Thomas Brown

Josh Whitman

Timothy Brown

James Green

Bryan Billings

Scott Black

Kyle Simon

Jonathan Groth

Daniel Young

Steven Black

girls

Kelsie Mitchell

Jill Green

Lisa Grove

Tiffany Brown

Melinda Briggs

Sally Black

Cassie Hartman

Amber White

✓ Jennifer Adams

Stephanie Black

Becka White

Sylvia Tyson

Jessica Green

Caitlin White

Mr. Jones's Class

1. *Adams, Jennifer*

2. _____

3. _____

4. _____

5. _____

6. _____

7. _____

8. _____

9. _____

10. _____

11. _____

12. _____

13. _____

14. _____

15. _____

16. _____

17. _____

18. _____

19. _____

20. _____

21. _____

22. _____

23. _____

24. _____

25. _____

26. _____

Bonus Box: Alphabetize *cycle, hors d'oeuvre, gym, school, tsunami, wrangle, gnash, phrase, gist,* and *gab* by the way they are pronounced—not by their spellings. Hint: *Phrase* (frāz) is first.

 The Best of The Mailbox® • Grades 4–6 • ©The Mailbox® Books • TEC61169 • Key p. 187

Welcome to Wackyland School!

Where in your classroom would you keep the dictionaries? Would you put them *in* your desk, *on* the shelves, or perhaps *alongside* the encyclopedias? Probably so. But students at Wackyland School keep their dictionaries *under* the plants, *behind* the clock, and *inside* the bathrooms!

A. Each italicized word above is a *preposition.* A preposition can tell where an object is located in relation to another object. After each school item listed below, write three different prepositional phrases that tell where it might be located in Wackyland School. Then circle the preposition in each phrase.

Example: the bulletin board (on) the ceiling, (under) the parking lot, (above) the roof

1. a student's desk _____
2. the school library _____
3. a report card _____

B. A preposition can also tell when something occurs. For example, a book may have been written either *before* or *after* your birth. Write a sentence about life at Wackyland School using each of the prepositions below.

4. during _____
5. after _____
6. until _____

C. Match each preposition on the apple with a group of words on the chalkboard to form a prepositional phrase. Write the phrases on the lines below. Then, on the back of this page, use each prepositional phrase in a sentence about Wackyland School.

without
behind
upon
throughout
over
between
toward
around

7. _____
8. _____
9. _____
10. _____
11. _____
12. _____
13. _____
14. _____

the cafeteria's cooks
the principal
the playground
our best teacher
recess
a classroom pet
the entire school
every student

Bonus Box: List on the back of this page at least four pairs of prepositions that are opposites, such as *up* and *down.* Write sentences using three of the pairs.

Tricky Treats

Read the story. On the lines below, write the name of the person(s) or thing(s) each numbered pronoun represents.

Three friends got a late start on trick-or-treating. **(1) They** had wanted to finish their homework first. Jimmy rang the first doorbell. "Trick or treat!" **(2) he** yelled. Mrs. Green opened the door. **(3) She** said, "Hi, kids! I only have two treats left, but **(4) you** can split **(5) them**." Mary knocked on the second door. **(6) She** screamed when a laughing clown answered the door. **(7) It** was only Mr. Smith. **(8) He** dresses up every year to give out treats. Then the friends hurried to Mr. Moore's old house. When they rang **(9) his** doorbell, a black cat yowled and darted by them. The kids dropped **(10) their** candy and ran all the way home!

1. _____ 2. _____

3. _____ 4. _____

5. _____ 6. _____ 7. _____

8. _____ 9. _____ 10. _____

Name _____

Coordinate graphing

Autumn Art

Plot and label the point for each ordered pair. Then connect the points in alphabetical order. The first one has been done for you.

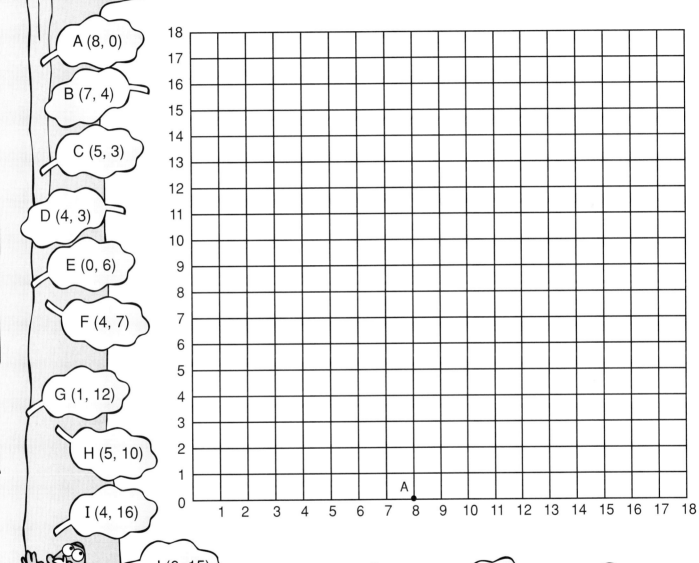

A (8, 0)

B (7, 4)

C (5, 3)

D (4, 3)

E (0, 6)

F (4, 7)

G (1, 12)

H (5, 10)

I (4, 16)

J (6, 15)

K (8, 18)

L (9, 15)

M (11, 16)

N (10, 11)

O (14, 12)

P (11, 6)

Q (14, 7)

R (11, 4)

S (9, 3)

T (8, 4)

U (9, 0)

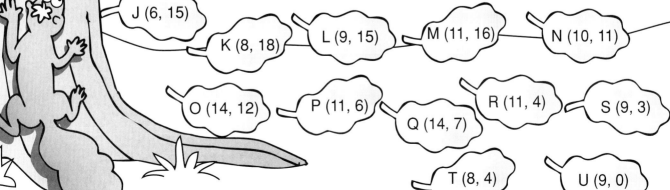

The Best of The Mailbox® • Grades 4–6 • ©The Mailbox® Books • TEC61169 • Key p. 187

81

The 12 Days of Math

Sing a round or so of "The 12 Days of Christmas" as you work these musical math problems! Show your work on another sheet of paper and then write your answers in the blanks provided. All of the gifts in the song are listed to help you. One more thing: You don't have 12 days to do these problems!

- a partridge in a pear tree
- 2 turtledoves
- 3 French hens
- 4 calling birds
- 5 gold rings
- 6 geese a-laying
- 7 swans a-swimming
- 8 maids a-milking
- 9 ladies dancing
- 10 lords a-leaping
- 11 pipers piping
- 12 drummers drumming

 1. There were 80 pears on the pear tree. One day the partridge became very excited about Christmas and knocked off $\frac{1}{2}$ of the pears. The next day he knocked off $\frac{1}{2}$ of the remaining pears. How many pears were left on the tree? _____

 2. The turtledoves were annoyed by all the leaping and drumming, so they decided to peck on the heads of the lords and drummers! How many heads must each dove peck? _____

 3. Suppose that all of the birds in the song are in your backyard. If you're blindfolded and select 1 bird, what are the chances that it will be a partridge? _____

 4. Each calling bird called 3 more calling birds to join the group. How many calling birds are there now? _____

 5. Each gold ring is worth $245.00. Each ring also includes a diamond worth $1,200.00. What is the total value of the 5 rings? _____

 6. The dancing ladies plan to share equally any eggs laid by the geese. Suppose each goose lays 1 egg a day for 30 days. How many eggs will each lady receive? _____

 7. How many more people than animals are included in the song? _____

 8. If each maid milked 3 cows a day, how many cows would the group milk in a week? _____

 9. The dancing ladies danced from 5:00 P.M. until 7:30 P.M. and then from 8:30 P.M. until midnight. How many hours in all did they dance? _____

 10. The dancing ladies and the leaping lords went to a fancy ball in fancy carriages. Each carriage holds 3 people. How many carriages were needed? _____

 11. If all the lords, pipers, and drummers are men, then how many more men than women are in the song? _____

 12. A pair of drumsticks costs $8.95 plus $0.45 tax. How much would it cost to buy each drummer a pair? _____

Bonus Box: Groups of drummers want to take groups of maids to a dance. What is the fewest number of groups of each that is needed so that everyone has a partner?

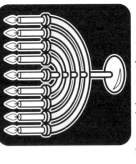

Shedding Light on Hanukkah

Hanukkah is an eight-night-long Jewish holiday. Read the passage below to find out more about it. Then match each boldfaced word to a definition by writing its number inside the appropriate candle. The words that come before and/or after each boldfaced word can help you determine its meaning.

Long ago, the Jewish city of Jerusalem was ruled by a **(1) dynasty.** One of the leaders of this dynasty was a man named Antiochus. Antiochus brought Greek **(2) culture** to Israel. He ordered the Jews to pay **(3) homage** to Greek gods and **(4) idols.** This went against the Jews' beliefs. When the Jews refused to give up their **(5) Judaism,** the armies of Antiochus **(6) desecrated** the Jewish temple. After seven years of fighting, the Jews got the temple back and **(7) purified** it.

A story in the **(8) Talmud** says that when the Jews got the temple back, they looked for oil to light the lamps. They found a **(9) vial** with enough oil to last for only one night. **(10) Miraculously,** the oil lasted for eight nights! Hanukkah **(11) commemorates** that event. To celebrate, the Jews light a new candle on a **(12) menorah** each night during Hanukkah.

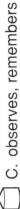

A. statues, pictures, or other objects that represent gods

B. small container

C. observes, remembers

D. damaged something so that it is no longer holy

E. candleholder used in Jewish worship

F. respect

G. Jewish holy book

H. religion of the Jewish people

I. in a way that suggests heavenly involvement

J. line of rulers who belong to the same family

K. made pure or clean

L. customs and beliefs of a group of people

Bonus Box: On the back of this paper, list in order the underlined letters in the boldfaced words. You'll spell the name of the special menorah candle that is used to light the other candles.

What If...?

I have a dream.

What if Martin Luther King Jr. were alive today? You probably know lots about Dr. King. He was a black civil rights leader who was born in 1929 and died in 1968. He was only 39 years old when he died. His birthday is celebrated each year as a tribute to his ideas on equal rights and nonviolence.

A lot has changed since the days of King's peaceful protests, but the world still needs equality and peace. Think about how Martin Luther King Jr. might affect our society if he were alive today. Read the questions on the right. Choose three to answer in short paragraphs. Write your paragraphs on another sheet of paper.

1. If Dr. King were alive today, what three main problems in our society do you think he would be trying to solve?

2. If he were alive today, do you think Dr. King would be holding a political office? If so, which one? If not, why not?

3. Which groups of people would Dr. King most likely be helping with equal rights today?

4. In his lifetime, Dr. King received many honorary university degrees. He was also chosen as *Time* magazine's Man of the Year for 1963. He won the Nobel Peace Prize in 1964. Dr. King was a minister, a speaker, and a respected civil rights leader. If he were teaching in a university today, what subjects do you think he might be teaching? Why?

5. If Dr. King were alive today, he would be happy with the progress made in some civil rights areas. Finish this paragraph starter, spoken by Dr. King: "I am so glad that…"

6. If Martin Luther King Jr. were alive today, do you think we would be celebrating his birthday this year? Why or why not?

Bonus Box: Dr. King gave his famous "I Have a Dream" speech in Washington, DC, in 1963. If he gave a speech today with the same title, what would it include? Write the opening paragraph of the speech.

Name_____ Combining sentences

Heart to Heart

You've heard of a heart-to-heart conversation, right? Well, now it's time for a little heart-to-heart combination! Read each pair of simple sentences. Decide which conjunction—*and, but,* or *or*—to use to combine the two sentences into a compound sentence. Write the conjunction in the numbered space. Then, on another sheet of paper, write each compound sentence.

Bonus Box: Create three heart-to-heart pairs of simple sentences that can be combined into compound sentences. Trade sentences with a partner. Then combine your partner's sentences to form compound sentences.

The Best of The Mailbox® • Grades 4–6 • ©The Mailbox® Books • TEC61169 • Key p. 187

85

This Could Be Your Lucky Number!

March 17 is a day that causes many people to think about good luck. See whether the number 17 is lucky for you!

Directions: Solve each problem. Then write your answer in the blank. If the answer is 17, color a coin in the pot yellow. Use a dictionary and a calculator if you need help.

1. Begin with the number of days in March. Subtract the value of the Roman numeral XI. Then subtract the number of sides in a triangle. _____

2. Start with the number of syllables in the word *leprechaun.* Add the number of days in two weeks. _____

3. Take the number of musicians in a quintet. Add to it the sum of $\frac{4}{6} + \frac{1}{3}$. Then double your answer. _____

4. Start with the numerator in $\frac{7}{10}$. Add to it the number of items in a baker's dozen. Then subtract the digit that is in the tens place in 936. _____

5. Begin with the number of quarters in $0.50. Multiply that number by a single-digit even number larger than 6. Then add to it the number of proboscises on an elephant. _____

6. Take the quotient of 24 ÷ 8. Add to it the perimeter of a 4' x 3' room. _____

7. Round 128 to the nearest hundred. Divide that number by the number of sides in a quadrilateral. Then subtract the number of arms on an octopus. _____

8. Start with the number of millimeters in three centimeters. Add to it the number of cardinal directions. Divide it by the number of inches in $\frac{1}{6}$ of a foot. _____

9. Take the number of thousands in 5,843. Multiply it by the number of *a*'s in *Saint Patrick's Day.* _____

10. Write one less than the number of shamrocks you see on this page. _____

Bonus Box: Create a problem of your own that has an answer of 17.

86 **Note to the teacher:** To complete this page, each child will need a yellow crayon or marker and access to a dictionary and calculator.

Name _____

The Earth Day Way

Write each fraction in simplest form.

1. $\frac{9}{27}$ = _____ (N)

2. $6\frac{4}{8}$ = _____ (A)

3. $3\frac{12}{16}$ = _____ (S)

4. $\frac{12}{24}$ = _____ (T)

5. $\frac{8}{36}$ = _____ (I)

6. $\frac{2}{8}$ = _____ (L)

7. $4\frac{3}{6}$ = _____ (E)

8. $5\frac{2}{8}$ = _____ (R)

9. $\frac{6}{15}$ = _____ (V)

10. $\frac{12}{16}$ = _____ (D)

11. $2\frac{6}{16}$ = _____ (G)

12. $\frac{16}{24}$ = _____ (O)

What can people do to make every day Earth Day?

To answer the question, write the letter of each problem above in its matching answer blank below.

$\overline{3\frac{3}{4}}$ $\overline{6\frac{1}{2}}$ $\overline{\frac{2}{5}}$ $\overline{4\frac{1}{2}}$ $\overline{4\frac{1}{2}}$ $\overline{\frac{1}{3}}$ $\overline{4\frac{1}{2}}$ $\overline{5\frac{1}{4}}$ $\overline{2\frac{3}{8}}$

Y and $\overline{\frac{3}{4}}$ $\overline{\frac{2}{3}}$ $\overline{\frac{1}{3}}$ $\overline{\frac{1}{2}}$, $\overline{\frac{1}{4}}$ $\overline{\frac{2}{9}}$ $\overline{\frac{1}{2}}$ $\overline{4\frac{1}{2}}$ $\overline{5\frac{1}{4}}$!

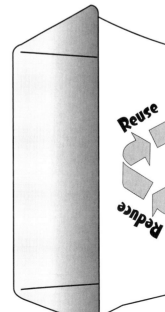

Reuse · Reduce · Recycle

The Best of The Mailbox® · Grades 4–6 · ©The Mailbox® Books · TEC61169 · Key p. 187

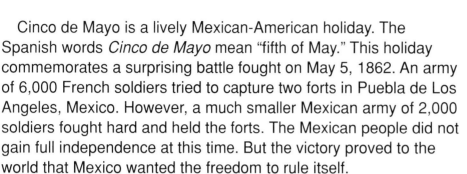

¡Celebrate Cinco de Mayo!

Cinco de Mayo is a lively Mexican-American holiday. The Spanish words *Cinco de Mayo* mean "fifth of May." This holiday commemorates a surprising battle fought on May 5, 1862. An army of 6,000 French soldiers tried to capture two forts in Puebla de Los Angeles, Mexico. However, a much smaller Mexican army of 2,000 soldiers fought hard and held the forts. The Mexican people did not gain full independence at this time. But the victory proved to the world that Mexico wanted the freedom to rule itself.

Want to learn more about how this fun-filled holiday is celebrated? Use your best detective skills to unscramble the sentences below. Be careful—there are five words that don't belong in the sentences. Just mark out those words. Then rewrite each sentence on another sheet of paper, using capital letters and punctuation correctly.

1. part many Americans in activities observe Cinco de Mayo fun take to
2. celebrate it's a people time to the of Mexico and friendship America between the
3. we parades and to speeches colorful valentines listen attend
4. white decorated red and are green in streets
5. red and the colors of the white Mexican green are flag
6. enjoy bunny people Mexican food traditional
7. include some of foods tortillas and special these guacamole
8. American special dances musical cities events are and held in many
9. famous guitars on musicians their sleigh play tunes
10. local play bands patriotic songs Mexican mask
11. around dancers twirl castanets and snap their
12. in last cities often for some several festivals days
13. Hall Los Angeles activities in the streets outside held City are in
14. the become a holiday has turkey celebration of heritage Hispanic

Bonus Box: Unscramble these popular Mexican foods: *ascto, drifeer nabes, tho lishice, norc saltirotl, daihensacl,* and *trobsiru.* Circle the foods you have tried.

The Spelling Bee

Unscramble each set of letters to spell a summertime word.

1. CAATOINV = __ __ __ __ __ __ __ __
   ₁

2. CEBHA = __ __ __ __ __
   ₂

3. UECABBRE = __ __ __ __ __ __ __ __
   ₃

4. IBRD GNIHCWTA = __ __ __ __ - __ __ __ __ __ __ __ __
   ₄

5. ECI MEARC = __ __ __   __ __ __ __ __
   ₅

6. EIRFKROSW = __ __ __ __ __ __ __ __ __
   ₆

7. TSELAACDNS = __ __ __ __ __ __ __ __ __ __
   ₇

8. LABESLAB = __ __ __ __ __ __ __ __
   ₈

9. ARTSOEABDK = __ __ __ __ __ __ __ __ __ __
   ₉

10. PCIMANG = __ __ __ __ __ __ __
    ₁₀

11. TOAINBG = __ __ __ __ __ __ __
    ₁₁

12. LLEESSSAH = __ __ __ __ __ __ __ __ __
    ₁₂

13. INSGWMIM OLOP = __ __ __ __ __ __ __ __   __ __ __ __
    ₁₃

14. STUNNA = __ __ __ __ __ __
    ₁₄

15. GNIHTAB ITSU = __ __ __ __ __ __ __   __ __ __ __
    ₁₅

Why does Honey Bee like to spell so much?

To solve the riddle, match the numbered letters above to the blanks below.

__ __   __ __ __ __ __   __ __ __   __ __ __ __
10 15   13 1 9 2 7   12 2 5   6 2 2 8

"__ __ - __ __ __ __ __ __ - __ __ __ __ __ __ " !
 4 10   7 15 10 14 11   3 10 7 12 2 4

Perfect Fit!

Multiply. Write the product in simplest terms. Then color the shoe with the matching answer. Some shoes will not be colored.

1. $\frac{3}{8} \times \frac{2}{5} =$

2. $\frac{6}{8} \times \frac{2}{9} =$

3. $\frac{4}{5} \times \frac{2}{3} =$

4. $\frac{2}{5} \times \frac{5}{6} =$

5. $\frac{6}{10} \times \frac{5}{8} =$

6. $\frac{8}{9} \times \frac{1}{7} =$

7. $\frac{2}{3} \times \frac{6}{9} =$

8. $\frac{4}{10} \times \frac{1}{2} =$

9. $\frac{3}{4} \times \frac{4}{6} =$

10. $\frac{1}{4} \times \frac{5}{9} =$

11. $\frac{1}{5} \times \frac{5}{10} =$

12. $\frac{3}{6} \times \frac{4}{8} =$

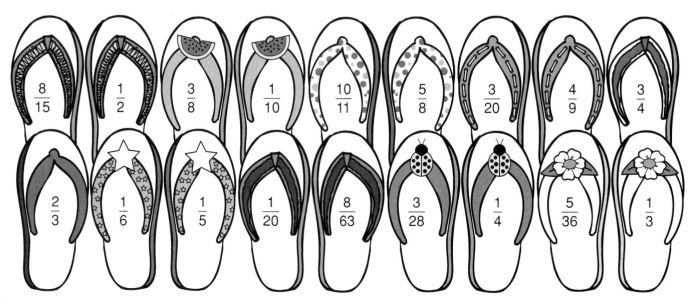

Write On!

Off to a Great Start
I am so excited about this school year! All summer long, I hoped I'd get the teacher I wanted, and I did! She really made us feel right at home. I'm excited about the things we'll be learning, the trips we'll be taking, and the projects we'll be doing. I look forward to coming to school every day. When this year is finally over, my friends and I will have learned so much our heads will be spinning!

Eli

School's cool!

"Purr-fect" Paragraphs
Reflective writing

Get your students back into the mode of basic paragraph writing with an activity that can become a delightful open house display! Have each child share what he likes about the school year thus far in a paragraph that includes a topic sentence, supporting details, and a conclusion. When his paragraph is ready to publish, instruct him to trim around the writing and then color and attach cutouts like the ones shown. For writers who want to embellish the cutouts, have colorful paper scraps on hand!

Teresa Vilfer-Snyder, Fredericktown Intermediate, Fredericktown, OH

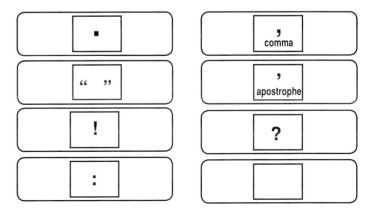

Almost a Disaster

Last Saturday, Mom asked Dad to hang a flagpole on our house. He fetched a ladder and all went well until he reached the top rung. He sneezed, dropped the pole, and lost his balance. Watch out! The ladder is falling! shouted Mom. She ran to hold the ladder. Fortunately she got there in time to catch the pole and steady the ladder. She told Dad to come down. We're still waiting for the flagpole to be hung!

Stellar Story Elements
Writing a narrative

Star-studded adventure stories will pour from your writing center when students are the ones contributing the key elements! On each of ten yellow star cutouts, write a brief general description of a different book or film character suggested by your students. In the same way, label each of ten blue star cutouts with a different problem or issue to be resolved and each of ten red star cutouts with a different story setting (see the examples). Each time a child visits the center, have her choose one star of each color and use the three elements to write a story. Even your most reluctant writers will be inspired!

Terry Healy
Marlatt Elementary
Manhattan, KS

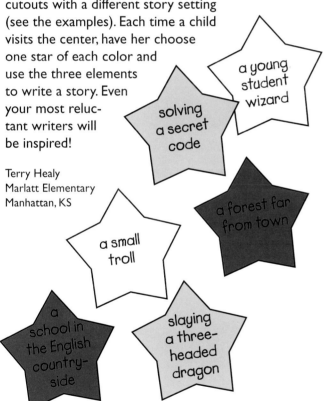

a young student wizard

solving a secret code

a forest far from town

a small troll

a school in the English countryside

slaying a three-headed dragon

Editing Aids
Correcting punctuation errors

Motivate your writers to correct the punctuation mistakes they make in sentences, paragraphs, or stories by attaching boo-boo strips to their papers! Each time you spot a punctuation mistake, use a glue stick to affix a copy of a label pattern below at the end of the line in which the mistake occurred. (Or copy the patterns on label paper.) Then return the paper to the child and have him correct the mistake the strip points out. To include other types of boo-boos, use the blank strip or cover the programming on the other patterns and add your own!

Janet Shipman, Hunt Elementary, Victoria, TX

.	, comma
" "	' apostrophe
!	?
:	

Hook Your Reader!
Writing lead sentences

Want to help your young writers create lead sentences that really reel their readers in? Then try this fishy activity:

1. Cut out five paper hooks and a supply of colorful fish cutouts. Write a different one of the following labels on each hook: "Question," "Onomatopoeia," "Interesting Fact," "Dialogue," "Description of Setting." Post the hooks on a bulletin board titled "Hook Your Reader!"
2. Discuss the types of leads shown on the board. Point out that a good lead acts like bait to hook a reader and encourage him to keep reading.
3. Divide the class into groups of five and give each group five fish cutouts. Assign each group a different topic, such as "The Best Day of Your Life." Then have group members label each fish cutout with a different type of lead sentence related to their topic.
4. Have each group read its sentences aloud. Challenge the class to identify the type of lead each sentence represents. Then have the group pin its cutouts on the board next to the appropriate hooks.

Encourage students to refer to the hooks when they're writing and need help baiting their readers.

Have you ever been so scared your knees were knocking?

Question

Amy Vanderwaall, Denham Oaks Elementary, Lutz, FL

OREO

Writing to Persuade

O = Opinion

R = Reason(s)

E = Explain (elaborate)

O = Opinion (restate)

Cookie Compositions
Persuasive writing

Use this sweet idea to improve persuasive-writing skills. First, label a poster with the steps shown and review the steps with students. Next, assign the class a topic, such as "What is the best pet?" Have each student use the OREO format to write a persuasive paragraph about the topic on a white paper circle. Then direct the writer to sandwich her story between two black paper circles and decorate the cover with a white or gray crayon. For inspiration, give each child an Oreo cookie to munch on as she works. Mmm, good!

Carrie L. Greene, Oakfield-Alabama Elementary, Oakfield, NY

Brown Bag Surprise
Descriptive writing

Bag descriptive-writing skills with this creative activity! Place an object, such as a piece of candy, in a small paper bag. Show students the bag. Then explain that you will use your five senses to describe an object inside. Start with a vague description, such as "My object is green. It is small." Give students five chances to guess the item. Then describe it again using more descriptive phrases, such as "My object is apple green and fits in the palm of my hand." Again, allow five guesses. Then discuss why the second description is better than the first. Continue giving more descriptive clues until someone identifies the object.

As a follow-up, give each student a paper bag to take home. Have him place an item from home in the bag and write a description of it. The next day, have each child share his description. If students cannot identify the object, allow the child to rewrite his description and try again the next day.

Amanda Holland and Mindy Adamonis, Longdale Elementary, Glen Allen, VA

Seasonal Snapshots
Descriptive writing

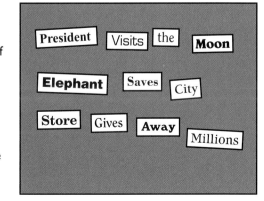

Imagine your students eager to try their hands at descriptive writing. It can happen with this motivating idea that's perfect for any season! Purchase two disposable cameras. Then have each student, in turn, take a camera home and snap two photos of an outdoor scene that illustrates some aspect of the current season. Encourage students to take pictures of unique images, such as a snowman melting in the January sun, dazzling icicles hanging from an icy rooftop, or a child pulling a sled up a snowy slope. After the film has been developed, give each child his photo and have him write a paragraph describing the scene. Or post the photos on a bulletin board titled "Seasonal Snapshots." Then have each student choose a classmate's photograph and write about its scene.

Kerri Drabek, Toledo, OH

| Don't just <u>walk</u> when you can… |
| Don't just <u>eat</u> when you can… |
| Don't just <u>say</u> it when you can… |
| Don't just <u>run</u> when you can… |
| Don't just <u>see</u> when you can… |
| Don't just <u>laugh</u> when you can… |

Present	Past	Future
saunter	sauntered	will saunter

Don't Just Run...
Word choice, verb tenses

Try this group activity to help students give boring verbs in their stories the boot! Divide the class into small groups. Give each group a sheet of chart paper labeled as shown. Then challenge each group to list in the chart's table at least two vivid present-tense verbs to replace each underlined verb. Provide dictionaries and thesauruses to help students. After the group lists the present-tense verbs, have students add the past and future forms as shown. Then have each group share its completed chart. Post the charts near a word wall or in your writing center. Encourage students to add to the charts throughout the year.

Amy Vanderwaall, Port Richey, FL

Making Headlines
Writing a newspaper story

Looking for a newsworthy way to help your students practice writing newspaper stories? You've just found it! Give each child the materials listed. Then set a timer for 15 minutes and challenge each student to cut out as many headlines as possible. When time is up, direct each student to cut apart the words in his headlines. Then guide students through the steps shown. Bind the finished stories to make a class book.

Materials for each student: 1–2 newspaper sections, scissors, 9" x 12" sheet of construction paper, sheet of notebook paper, glue stick, pencil

1. On your desktop, create as many new headlines as possible using the words you cut out. Be creative!
2. Glue each new headline on the construction paper.
3. Glue the notebook paper to the back of the construction paper.
4. Choose your favorite headline and write a newspaper story to go with it. Be sure to answer the following questions in your story: Who? What? Where? When? Why? How? Write your story on the notebook paper.

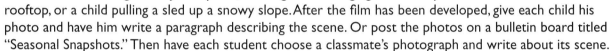

Joyce Hovanec, Glassport Elementary, Glassport, PA

Tag Team Revisions
Peer-editing

Passing a paper tag can turn revising students' story writing into a team effort! Make, label, and laminate several poster board tags as shown. When students are ready to revise their writing, divide them into groups of four. Give one student in the group a tag and have that student read her paper to her three group mates. After she reads, have her hand the tag to any child in the group. Direct the recipient of the tag to identify a part of the story that is unclear and then pass the tag to another group member. Have that child ask the writer to clarify something about the story and then pass the tag to the remaining group member. Instruct this student to suggest an improvement. The writer records each person's feedback and uses it to revise her story. This continues until each student has received feedback. Go, team!

T–Tell about a part of the story that is unclear.
A–Ask a question to clarify something.
G–Give a suggestion for improvement.

April Dennis, Meadowlane Elementary, West Melbourne, FL

On Friday, I was resting inside Ms. Markland's desk when I heard her announce a field trip. I almost toppled over with excitement! Surely she would take me along and later put my p[...] in a scrapbook. But then [I] thought, "What if she tak[es] the digital camera inste[ad] and I miss all the fun?" [I was] so worried, my flash al[most] went off!

That's me!

First-Person Perspectives
Writing to show first-person point of view

What do you get when you mix mystery, a classroom object, and first-person point of view? A fun writing lesson! Ask each student to think of a classroom object and a situation that could involve the object. Then have the child write a paragraph or story about the event from the object's point of view without revealing what the object is. When everyone is finished, invite each writer to share his work while the class tries to guess the object's identity.

Heather Kime Markland, Chatham Park Elementary, Havertown, PA

SHOW Me a Summary!
Writing a summary

Make summarizing as easy as spelling S-H-O-W! Create a transparency of a brief newspaper article. (Enlarge the text if necessary.) Also make and display a poster of the acronym shown. Next, display the transparency and read the text aloud. Then summarize the article for the class, using the acronym as a guide. Follow up by having each child use the SHOW method to summarize a particular section from his social studies or science text or a short passage of his reading text. Who would have thought that four little letters could make a tough task so easy to do?

Sugar Thiessen, Grace Abbott Elementary, Omaha, NE

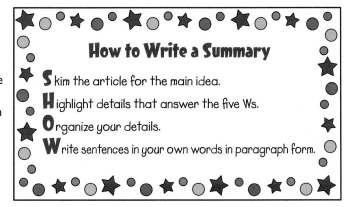

How to Write a Summary

S kim the article for the main idea.

H ighlight details that answer the five Ws.

O rganize your details.

W rite sentences in your own words in paragraph form.

"Auto-biographical" Stories
Narrative writing

Looking for an activity that "vrooms" in on narrative-writing skills? Instruct each student to pretend that he is the family car or truck. Then give each child a copy of page 99, scissors, three or four sheets of lined paper, and crayons, markers, or colored pencils. (You'll also need a stapler.) Have each student complete the page as directed to write an "auto-biographical" story about an interesting event in his life as an auto. To help students complete Step 5, explain that a *ghostwriter* is someone who writes for and in the name of another. Pin the finished story booklets on a bulletin board titled "Awesome 'Auto-biographical' Tales." For a fun finishing touch, have students add to the display pictures of cars and trucks that they've cut from old newspapers and magazines.

Colleen Dabney, Williamsburg, VA

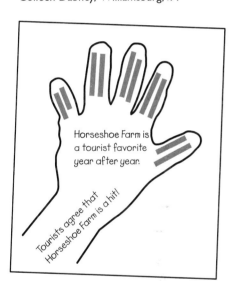

Handy Paragraph Planner
Prewriting, writing a paragraph

Help your students plan top-notch paragraphs using a "hand-y" graphic organizer. Before a student writes an assigned paragraph, have her trace her hand and wrist on a sheet of paper. Then have her label each part of the hand as follows:

Palm: Topic sentence identifying the paragraph's subject

Fingers and thumb: On each digit, a sentence with details that make the subject interesting and clear

Wrist: Closing sentence that reminds readers of the subject and keeps them thinking about it

After completing the organizer, a student will be ready to write a well-planned paragraph. How "hand-y"!

Pamela Hilton, Dolvin Elementary, Alpharetta, GA

Sentence Skylines
Writing varied sentences

Use this unique activity to help your students write sentences that vary in structure and length. Ask your librarian to supply you with pictures of city skylines. Share the pictures with students. Point out that varied sentences add interest to a writing piece in the same way that a variety of buildings add character to a city's skyline. End the discussion by having each student write the first draft of a short writing assignment.

Next, provide each child with a 12" x 18" sheet of construction paper, construction paper scraps, a ruler, scissors, and glue. Direct the student to create a building to represent each sentence. The catch? Students can only vary a building's design from the other buildings if the sentence it represents differs from the other sentences in the composition. Encourage each student to revise his draft as he works to create an interesting skyline. When a child is pleased with his draft, have him glue his cutouts to the paper. Then let him add details with fine-tip markers or colored pencils. Display the projects and the written pieces on a class clothesline or bulletin board with the title "Sentence Skylines."

Jane Cabourg, Haworth Public School, Haworth, NJ

At the park, I noticed a door under the slide. When I pushed it open...

$100

What's Behind the Door?
Prewriting, narrative writing

Knock, knock! Who's there? An easy-to-adapt writing activity! Cover a classroom door with butcher paper. Label the top of the paper with an intriguing prompt about a door (see the example). Then place a container of markers or crayons nearby. When a student finishes her classwork, let her draw on the paper what she thinks is behind the mysterious door.

After several days, discuss the pictures students have drawn on the door. Then have each child use the doorway mural to gather ideas for a narrative piece about the prompt. Provide time for students to share their stories. Then cover the door again and display a new prompt. Vary the prompts to practice different types of writing, such as descriptive, expository, or even poetry!

Adrienne Ambrose, Holly Hill Elementary, Holly Hill, FL

Let's Get Cookin'!
Expository writing

Cook up a fun way to practice expository writing with this cool activity! Have each student bring in an empty food product container, such as boxes of pasta, cake mix, or pudding. Require that the container feature preparation directions. Then direct each student to follow these steps:
1. Use the directions on your package to write an expository paragraph that explains how to prepare the food.
2. Add at least three extra details to the directions. For example, add, "Be sure to turn the pot's handle away from the front of the stove."
3. Add a catchy opening sentence that will hook the reader and a concluding sentence that wraps up the paragraph.
4. Have a partner review your draft. Make any revisions and write the final copy on a clean sheet of paper.

Display each paragraph on a bulletin board alongside its container. If space is limited, place each paragraph inside its container on the display.

Doreen Placko, St. Patrick School, Wadsworth, IL

My Own Poetry Pattern
Writing poetry, creative thinking

Wrap up a study of poetry with a challenging creative-writing project. Review with the class different forms of poetry, such as cinquain, haiku, couplet, limerick, and quatrain. Then challenge students (or small groups) to create their own poetry styles. Instruct each child to explain her style on chart paper, including a sample poem. Then have her share her chart with the class. As an extension, post the students' charts around the room. Then ask each child to choose a favorite pattern and write a poem that uses it. Direct the student to copy the poem on a construction paper cutout that represents the poem's subject. Then display the finished poetry on a bulletin board titled "Our Personal Poetry Patterns."

Dina Hardt, Orchard Hills School, Milford, CT

Shelley's Poetry Pattern
your first name
two adverbs that describe you
three -ing action verbs that
    describe you doing something
four adjectives that describe you
three nicknames for you
two color words that represent you
your last name

Shelley
impatiently, happily
dancing, singing, smiling
energetic, athletic, moody, kind
Sweet Pea, Shelley Belle, Smiley
orange, pink
Winkler

Turn to page 100 to find a fun-to-do reproducible on writing with onomatopoeia!

An "Auto-biographical" Story

Pretend that you are your family car or another vehicle in which you've ridden. Then write an "auto-biographical" account about an interesting event in your life on the road. Follow these steps:

1. Staple two sheets of lined paper behind this page.
2. Answer the questions below on the first sheet of paper.
3. Write your first draft on the second sheet of paper.
4. Revise and edit your draft.
5. Fill in the lines on the gas pump. Color and cut out the pump.
6. Trace the gas pump on lined paper and cut out the tracings. Write your final copy on the paper and staple it behind the gas pump at the Xs.

Beginning
1. Who was involved in the event?
2. Where and when did the story take place?

Middle
3. What important or exciting thing happened?

Ending
4. What did you learn from the experience?
5. How did you feel afterward?

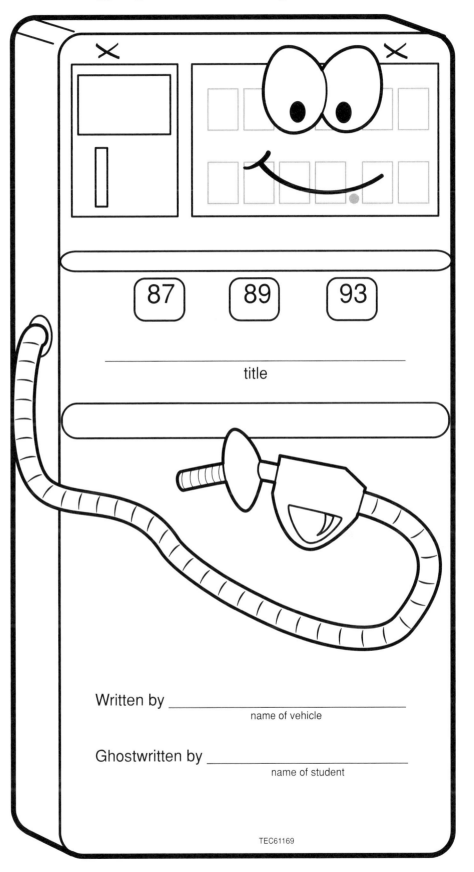

87   89   93

_____
title

Written by _____
name of vehicle

Ghostwritten by _____
name of student

TEC61169

Note to the teacher: Use with "'Auto-biographical' Stories'" on page 97. Each student will need scissors, access to a stapler, three or four sheets of lined paper, and crayons, markers, or colored pencils to complete this page.

Sounds Good to Me!

Onomatopoeia is the use of words that sound like their meanings. For example, *buzz* and *boom* are examples of onomatopoeia. Below each picture, write a matching example of onomatopoeia from the box. Then, on the back of this page, write a sentence about the picture using the onomatopoeia word.

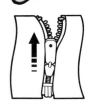

drip	tap	tinkle	clang	crash
hum	zip	rat-a-tat	jangle	bang
pop	crunch	hiss	thump	boom
swish				squeak

　　　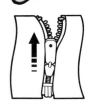

1. _____　2. _____　3. _____　4. _____

　　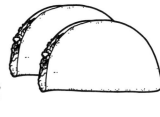　

5. _____　6. _____　7. _____　8. _____

9. _____　10. _____　11. _____　12. _____

Bonus Box: On another sheet of paper, write a descriptive or narrative paragraph that uses at least three of the onomatopoeia words above.

Language Arts Units

Punctuation Rules!

Try these royally fun activities and watch your classroom become a place where proper punctuation rules!

by Simone Lepine, Gillette Road Middle School, Cicero, NY

Pick a Corner, Any Corner
Ending punctuation, kinds of sentences

Challenge your students to think on their feet with a "grammarvelous" review of ending punctuation rules! Make the four posters shown. Then mount each poster in a different corner of your classroom. Next, review the four kinds of sentences—declarative, imperative, interrogative, and exclamatory—and the ending punctuation mark for each kind. After the review, have each student write one sentence of any kind on an index card. Then collect the cards and follow these steps:

1. Instruct each student to choose a corner and stand in it.
2. Read aloud one sentence. Ask a volunteer to identify the correct kind of sentence and ending punctuation. Discuss the sentence with students. Then ask everyone standing in that corner to sit down.
3. Direct the remaining standing students to decide whether to stay in their original corners or move to different ones. At your signal, have students who wish to change corners do so.
4. After each standing student has chosen a corner, repeat Steps 2–3. Continue until only one child is left standing. If you run out of sentences before declaring a winner, ask volunteers from the sitting students to suggest new ones to use.

Positive Pat Meets Negative Nell
Using apostrophes in contractions

Invite a couple of cutouts into your classroom to help students review how to use apostrophes in contractions. Cut two large paper-doll shapes from construction paper and decorate them as shown. Introduce the dolls to students as Positive Pat and Negative Nell. Explain that Pat has a positive attitude and always says things such as "I *will* do my homework" or "I *could* help my sister." But Negative Nell has a negative attitude and always changes Pat's sentences by using contractions, such as "I *won't* do my homework" or "I *couldn't* help my sister." Point out that each contraction is made by leaving out one or more letters from the original words (such as *will not*) and replacing them with an apostrophe.

Next, divide the class into pairs. Challenge each twosome to write four pairs of statements that Pat and Nell might make, using the words on the paper dolls to help them (see Example 1). When each pair has completed its sentences, have the students share their work with the class or another twosome. If desired, use Pat and Nell to teach students how to punctuate dialogue too (see Example 2).

Example 1
Pat: I could help my sister.
Nell: I couldn't help my sister.

Example 2
Pat said, "I could help my sister."
"I couldn't help my sister," replied Nell.

Punctuating Possessives
Using apostrophes in possessives, subject-verb agreement

Using apostrophes correctly can be tricky for students if they're confused about possessive nouns. Clear up any confusion with a partner activity that also tackles subject-verb agreement.

Materials for each student pair: 40 paper clips, scissors, copy of page 105, paper and pencils, copy of the answer key on page 188

Steps:
1. Cut out the cards on page 105. Separate the noun and *s* cards into two stacks.
2. Pretend that the paper clips are apostrophes. Draw a noun card and decide whether the noun is singular or plural. Then make the noun possessive by either clipping an *s* to the card or by attaching only a paper clip as shown.
3. When all words have been made possessive, check with the key. Correct any errors.
4. Group each singular possessive with its matching plural possessive (example: *children's* and *child's*).
5. Choose ten pairs of words. For each pair, write two sentences like the example shown, making sure the nouns and verbs agree.

Example:	The <u>child's</u> toy was bright red.
	The <u>children's</u> toys were bright red.

Absurd Appositives
Punctuating appositives

Just as salt seasons a dull dish, a wacky sentence or two can liven up any grammar assignment—as proven by this three-part activity on punctuating with appositives! Complete the activity in three mini lessons or one longer session.

Part 1: Review declarative sentences with students. Then have each child list five friends or family members on his paper. Beside each name, have the student list something that person enjoys doing. Then have him write a declarative sentence that states the person's name and favorite activity (see the example), skipping two or three lines after the sentence. Tell students not to include appositives (such as *my sister*) in their sentences. Have the student repeat the steps for the other four people listed on his paper. Collect the papers.

> Mary likes to draw horses.

Part 2: Review with students common nouns and adjectives. Then have each student label a sheet of paper as shown. Have students brainstorm common nouns to list on the right sides of their papers. Then have them fold their papers to conceal the nouns and list adjectives (including the articles *a* or *an*) on the left sides. Collect the finished charts.

Adjectives	Nouns
1. a cuddly	hamburger
2. an orange	rabbit
3. a gigantic	kitten
4. a frightened	crab
5. a scarlet	bottle
6.	
7.	
8.	
9.	
10.	
11.	
12.	
13.	
14.	
15.	

Part 3: Return the papers completed in Part 2 to students. Review how to use commas to set off appositives. Then randomly distribute the papers collected in Part 1, making sure no child gets his own paper. Direct each student to use an adjective and noun from the chart he made in Part 2 to create an appositive. Then, on the lines below the first sentence, have him write a new sentence that includes the appositive (see the example). Have students repeat the steps for the remaining four sentences. Then ask each student to share his favorite silly sentence with the class.

> 1. Mary likes to draw horses.
>   *Mary, an orange rabbit, likes to draw horses.*
>
> 2.

Comical Conversations
Using quotation marks

Punctuating dialogue is no laughing matter, but you *can* make it a lot more fun with this activity! Ask your media specialist to provide you with several grade-level-appropriate joke and riddle books. Read a knock-knock joke or other riddle aloud to students. Then model for them how to rewrite it as a conversation, adding the appropriate punctuation (see the example). After completing several models together, divide the class into small groups. Give each group a marker, a sheet of chart paper, and one or more joke books. Challenge the group to select one or more jokes and rewrite them on the chart paper as conversations, checking their punctuation carefully. After each group has rewritten at least two jokes, have it share its comical conversations with the class.

> Tracy said, "Knock, knock."
> "Who's there?" asked Mary.
> "Ben," answered Tracy.
> Mary replied, "Ben who?"
> Tracy said, "Been knocking on your door all
>   afternoon!"
>
> John asked, "Why is 6 afraid of 7?"
> "Because 7 ate 9!" yelled Mike.

A Few of My Favorite Things
Writing and punctuating compound sentences

Use this kid-pleasin' activity to familiarize students with the punctuation of compound sentences—and with each other! First, review how to punctuate a compound sentence with a comma. After the review, have the class decide on three "favorites" questions, such as the ones shown. List the questions on the board. Then have students mill around the room and ask each other the three questions. Require that each child interview at least five classmates and that she write the interviewees' names and answers on her paper. When each student has completed her interviews, have her return to her desk. Then instruct the student to use her notes to write five compound sentences (see the example). When students finish, have them share their favorite sentences with the class.

> What is your favorite television program?
> What is your favorite food?
> What is your favorite activity to do after school?

> Kathleen likes to draw after school, but Tommy likes to ride his bike.

3-D Punctuation
Punctuating sentences

With just a few simple props, you can turn punctuation practice into a hands-on activity students will ask for again and again! Gather the items listed in the box. Also choose five to ten sentences that include the punctuation marks you want to review. Write each word of a sentence on a separate index card. Then place each sentence's cards inside a folded sheet of paper labeled with the sentence.

Next, pass out the cards for the first sentence and the props. Read the sentence aloud. Then challenge students holding the word cards to reconstruct the sentence at the front of the room. Invite the students holding props to insert the needed ones correctly in the sentence (see the illustration). Help the rest of the class evaluate the sentence and direct classmates on how to make any corrections. Then collect the cards, redistribute the props, and repeat the activity with another set of cards.

Who are you asked Ted

exclamation mark = broom
period = tennis ball
question mark = hooked cane (or a coat hanger bent as shown)
colon = two tennis balls, one held over the other
commas = ladles (two or three; ask the cafeteria staff for help)
quotation marks = four large pipe cleaners, slightly bent, to make one set

Use with "Punctuating Possessives" on page 103.

teacher TEC61169	deer TEC61169	mother TEC61169	boss TEC61169
teachers TEC61169	deer TEC61169	mothers TEC61169	bosses TEC61169
child TEC61169	baby TEC61169	secretary TEC61169	fox TEC61169
children TEC61169	babies TEC61169	secretaries TEC61169	foxes TEC61169
man TEC61169	woman TEC61169	principal TEC61169	radio TEC61169
men TEC61169	women TEC61169	principals TEC61169	radios TEC61169
puppy TEC61169	student TEC61169	house TEC61169	monkey TEC61169
puppies TEC61169	students TEC61169	houses TEC61169	monkeys TEC61169
goose TEC61169	wolf TEC61169	bus TEC61169	calf TEC61169
geese TEC61169	wolves TEC61169	buses TEC61169	calves TEC61169

s	s	s	s	s	s	s	s	s	s	s	s	s
s	s	s	s	s	s	s	s	s	s	s	s	s

PRESENTING THE MAIN EVENT

Turn the spotlight on main idea with these big top activities!

with ideas by Tina Cassidy, Ella Canavan Elementary, Medina, OH

Traveling Paragraphs
Determining details to support a main idea

Give students plenty of practice writing supporting details for main ideas with this round-robin group activity. Write on the board the main-idea sentences shown and then divide students into groups of five. Direct each group member to choose a different sentence from the board and write it at the top of his paper. Next, give each student one minute to write a supporting detail for his main idea. When time is up, instruct him to trade papers with another group member. Give the student another minute to read this new main idea and its detail and to add a different supporting detail. Then have him trade papers again. Continue in this manner until each student has written a supporting detail for all five ideas and traded to get his original paper back. Finally, have each student edit the resulting paragraph on his paper and share it with his group.

Main-Idea Sentences
The weather looked threatening.
The children had a great time at the party.
Marissa was a good student.
Jake's mother knew he wasn't feeling well.
The pizza was delicious.
Susan and Ashley were best friends.
Fall is a beautiful time of year.
The soccer game was very exciting.
The field trip was a great success.
The principal of the school was very kind.

I. Animal Behaviors and Adaptations
  A. Migration
    1. Migration happens when animals move back and forth from one region to another.
    2. Some animals migrate to lay eggs and raise babies.
    3. Other animals migrate to find a better climate and more food.
  B. Hibernation

Outline the Facts
Identifying main idea and supporting details in text, making an outline

Make main ideas and supporting details easier for students to spot with this colorful outlining activity. Divide students into small groups. Have each group read a different paragraph from the same chapter of a science or social studies textbook. Then give each group a colored sentence strip (the same color for each group) to label with the main idea of its paragraph. Have the group label several sentence strips of another color with supporting details as shown. Ask each group, in turn, to read its paragraph aloud and tape the main-idea and supporting-detail strips to the board, indenting them under a written topic as shown. Finally, help students add Roman numerals, capital letters, and numbers to complete the outline.

Information Webs
Finding supporting details in informational text

Show students how to snare supporting details from informational text with this web activity. First, have each student choose a subject to research in an encyclopedia (one that has at least three subheadings). Next, give each student one white 3" x 5" index card and a supply of index cards in two different colors. Instruct the student to write the title of his subject on the white card, the subheadings on the cards of one color, and the supporting details on the cards of the other color. Have students attach the subheading cards to the subject card and the supporting-detail cards to the subheading cards with small strips of construction paper as shown. Display several graphic organizers at a time on a bulletin board titled "Get Caught in Our Information Webs!"

Pattern

The Best of The Mailbox® • Grades 4–6 •
©The Mailbox® Books • TEC61169

Distinguishing main ideas from supporting details, writing a paragraph

Set the stage for distinguishing main ideas from supporting details with this paragraph-building activity. First, enlarge the cube pattern shown to fit a sheet of 8½" x 11" paper (or construction paper) and then make a copy for each student. Also have each student write a six-sentence paragraph.

Next, divide students into groups of six. Give each child scissors, tape, and a copy of the pattern. Direct the student to write the first sentence of her paragraph in any box on her pattern and then pass the pattern to her left. Then have her read the sentence on the pattern she receives, add a second sentence to one of its boxes, and pass it on. Have students continue in this manner until all the patterns' boxes have been labeled. Then have each group cut out its six cubes, fold them on the dotted lines, and tape them closed. Finally, instruct the group to construct one complete paragraph at a time by stacking the cubes, as shown, with the main-idea sentence at the top, two supporting details in the middle, and two supporting details and a concluding sentence at the base. Have the paragraph's author check the arrangement for accuracy before the group uses the cubes to build another paragraph.

In the News
Identifying the main ideas of newspaper articles

What's in the news? A great opportunity to practice identifying main ideas! Give each student two sheets of construction paper, scissors, glue, and a section from a newspaper. Instruct the student to cut out two articles. Have her glue each article's headline to one side of a sheet of construction paper and its corresponding article to the back. Then laminate the sheets. Next, pair students and give each twosome four articles turned headline side down. Instruct the pair to read each article, guess its headline, and then turn the sheet over to check. If desired, place the sheets in a center for students to use during their free time. For even more practice with this skill, give each student a copy of page 108 to complete as directed.

Hot off the Press!

The newspaper editor was in such a hurry to go to print that he forgot to write headlines for the articles below! Read each article. Then, on the lines provided, write the main idea of each one plus a catchy headline to grab the reader's attention.

| VOL. 30 No. 15 | **The Main Event** | 50 CENTS |

Headline: _____

_____

   Enormous the Elephant escaped from the circus train last Friday night and is running loose in Townsville. Peanut stands have been raided and cars and park benches have been smashed flat. If you happen to spot Enormous, please phone the authorities. Do not try to capture her on your own. She is considered trunked and dangerous!

Main idea: _____

_____

_____

Headline: _____

_____

   A medical research team surprised everyone yesterday by announcing the existence of a fifth food group—circus foods. The announcement said that cotton candy and ice cream are nutritious and part of a healthy diet. Other foods in this new group include hot dogs, elephant ears (similar to doughnuts), and lollipops. The medical community is questioning this study and its researchers, Dr. Barnum and Dr. Bailey. The researchers, however, are sticking to the story and denying the claims that their study has anything to do with their ownership of the circus and its concession stands.

Main idea: _____

_____

_____

Headline: _____

_____

   Joe B. Hedded, a famous lion tamer, had a terrible accident yesterday. It seems that as Mr. Hedded was practicing his trick of placing his head into a lion's mouth, the lion mistook him for dinner and bit down. Other circus members rushed over to help him, but the lion held firmly to Mr. Hedded's head for over an hour until someone finally located a crowbar and pried him loose. Mr. Hedded blames his new shampoo, Essence à la Steak, for the accident.

Main idea: _____

_____

_____

Headline: _____

_____

   Two circus performers want to get married while performing trapeze stunts on opening night. They have not had time to book a church because of their busy circus schedules. "We just thought, 'Why not get married in midair?'" said trapeze artist Michael Fly. His fiancée, Janie Glider, plans to wear the traditional white dress and veil as she swings on the trapeze. "Now, all we have to do is find a minister who is not afraid of heights!" the couple remarked.

Main idea: _____

_____

_____

Bonus Box: Write a newspaper article about something happening in your town. Have a classmate think of a headline that captures its main idea.

Taking Aim at Adjectives

Without adjectives, writing would be dull, dreary, and downright dreadful! Show your students how to use this indispensable part of speech effectively with the following on-target ideas!

by Marcia Barton, Cocoa Beach, FL

| The | blonde | boy | threw | the | beach | ball | to | his | little | sister. |

Adjective Additions
Using adjectives

Use this easy-to-do activity to show students how adjectives can turn a weak sentence into a winner. Write each word in the sentences at the right on a separate index card. Clip words in the same sentence together. Next, tape the cards for one sentence on the chalkboard. Give each student a blank index card and a marker or crayon. Then ask one child to write on his card an adjective that will make the sentence more interesting. Have the student tape his card on the board, rearranging cards as needed, and read the new sentence aloud. Then have him choose a classmate to add another adjective. Continue in this manner until three (or more) adjectives have been added. Then post another sentence and repeat the activity. Continue until each student has contributed an adjective. If desired, keep the practice going by posting a sentence on a classroom wall. Encourage early finishers to add adjective cards to the sentence during their free time. Then read the improved sentence together before dismissal and post the next day's sentence.

- The boy threw the ball to his sister.
- A kitten played in the garden with a butterfly.
- Fish swam in the lake.
- Rosie saw a pig in the barn.
- The lady gave a flower to the girl.
- The dog chased the squirrel up a tree.
- The rain fell in puddles on the sidewalk.

Targeting Types of Adjectives
Using common, proper, and demonstrative adjectives

Target different types of adjectives with this wet and wild class game! Begin by reviewing common, proper, and demonstrative adjectives. After the review, draw a large target on the board, as shown, and divide students into two teams. Use masking tape to mark a line about ten feet from the board. Have both teams line up behind the line. Then play a game of Adjective Target according to the rules listed below. (For a related activity, see the reproducible on page 111.)

Materials: small damp sponge, chalkboard, chalk, masking tape

How to play:
1. Player 1 on Team A tosses the sponge at the target. If he doesn't hit the target, his turn is over. If he does hit the target, the first player on Team B announces a noun. Then Player 1 on Team A adds to the noun an adjective that matches the type hit by the sponge. For example, if the sponge landed within the "proper" ring and the opponent's noun is *noodles,* Player 1 might respond, "Chinese noodles."
2. If Player 1 from Team A is incorrect, no points are scored. If Player 1 is correct, he scores the number of points indicated in the target. Then Player 1 on Team B throws the sponge and Player 2 on Team A names a noun.
3. Continue in this manner until each student has had a turn to throw the sponge or time runs out. Declare the team with more points the winner.

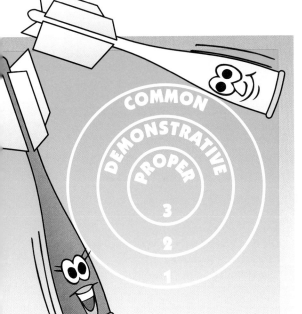

COMMON
DEMONSTRATIVE
PROPER
3
2
1

109

Window Words
Using colorful adjectives

For this weekly activity on using colorful adjectives, all you need is a clean window and a few broad-tipped dry-erase markers. On Monday, use one of the markers to write on the window a common or proper noun (see the list of suggestions shown). Challenge students to use their free time to add adjectives to the window graffiti-style (using a color of marker different from the noun). On Wednesday morning, review the words with the class, asking student volunteers to use the noun and each adjective in a sentence. Then challenge students to use the window words in their journal entries or other writing assignments during the rest of the week. Before dismissal on Friday, have a student wipe the window clean with a paper towel. Then write another noun on the window and repeat the activity the following week.

Common nouns: party, ocean, rocket, gift, cookie, flower, sky, song, pen, puppy, house, car

Proper nouns: names of famous pop or sports stars, favorite book characters, local or professional sports teams, foreign countries

Good, Better, Best Game
Using positive, comparative, and superlative adjectives

Looking for a good way to practice comparison of adjectives? There's no better activity than the following game! Review the rules for comparing adjectives shown below. Then divide the class into two teams and play by the rules listed.

Materials: index cards labeled with the positive adjectives listed in the box below (one word per card), paper bag

How to play:
1. Place the cards in the bag.
2. Have Player 1 from Team A draw a card and write its adjective on the board. Then have him write the comparative form of the adjective.
3. If Player 1 is incorrect, the first player on Team B gets a chance to provide the correct answer. If Player 1 is correct, he scores a point for his team and earns the right to list the superlative form on the board.
4. If Player 1 incorrectly lists the superlative form, the first player on Team B gets a chance to provide the correct answer. If Player 1 is correct, he scores a point for his team and his turn is over.
5. The game continues in this manner until time is up or all cards have been played. Declare the team with more points the winner.

Adjectives: bad, bright, friendly, beautiful, small, noisy, busy, smooth, tidy, gigantic, grumpy, handsome, itchy, magnificent, nutritious, ordinary, wasteful, wonderful, tender, brave, wise, big, safe, good, interesting, mysterious, jittery, ugly

Rules for Comparing Adjectives

1. Add -er and -est to short adjectives of one syllable (and sometimes two syllables).

sweet	sweeter	sweetest

2. If a short adjective ends with an e, add r and st.

cute	cuter	cutest

3. If a one- or two-syllable adjective ends with a consonant and y, change the y to i and add -er and -est.

pretty	prettier	prettiest

4. Use more and most in front of longer adjectives that have two, three, or more syllables.

wonderful	more wonderful	most wonderful
careful	more careful	most careful

5. Some adjectives have special forms to make comparisons.

good	better	best
bad	worse	worst

Targeting Adjectives

Take aim at adjectives by following the directions below!

Part 1: Underline each adjective in the sentences below. Do not underline any articles *(a, an,* or *the).*

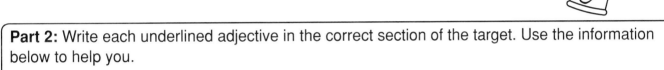

1. The warm apple pie was everyone's favorite dessert.

2. That French restaurant always has a long line of hungry customers.

3. He wrote a popular book about alien spaceships that invaded Earth.

4. This homework assignment took me two hours to complete.

5. Mom bought Idaho potatoes, Swiss cheese, and Spanish rice.

6. Irish music could be heard from inside the crowded concert hall.

7. Those basketball players can hardly fit into that tiny car.

8. We performed Mexican dances during the spring program.

Part 2: Write each underlined adjective in the correct section of the target. Use the information below to help you.

Demonstrative adjectives point out nouns.
> *this* book
> *those* cows

Common adjectives describe a noun in a general way.
> *cool* drink
> *grumpy* baby

Proper adjectives are made from proper nouns and are always capitalized.
> *Chinese* noodles
> *Asian* elephant

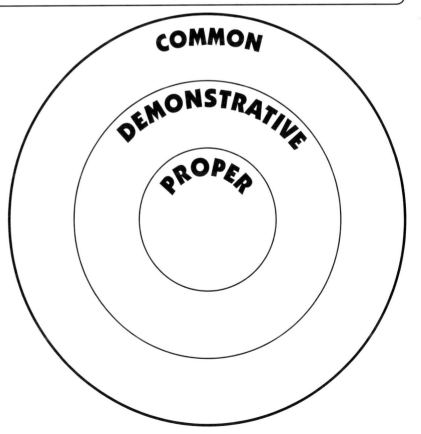

Bonus Box: Write three sentences about the silliest thing you ever did. Use at least three adjectives in your sentences. Underline the adjectives.

Note to the teacher: Use alone or with "Targeting Types of Adjectives" on page 109.

High-Flying Sentences

Watch students' skills with sentence structure soar with this sky-high collection of activities on simple, compound, and complex sentences!

by Julia Ring Alarie, Williston, VT

Simply Delicious!
Writing simple sentences

Whet students' appetites for writing simple sentences with this tasty activity. Begin by reviewing with students that a simple sentence has one complete thought but can include compound subjects, predicates, and phrases. Afterward, ask each child to list the foods she would most like to eat for breakfast, lunch, and dinner. Next, direct her to write a simple descriptive sentence about each of her favorite foods. Then give the student a sheet of 9" x 12" construction paper and have her fold it in thirds. Instruct her to copy her sentences in each section, as shown, and decorate it to create her own menu of favorites. Display the menus with the title "Simply Delicious Sentences!"

Breakfast

The scrambled eggs are fluffy and yellow.
I put extra butter on my toast.
Two strips of crispy bacon taste great with scrambled eggs.
Regular milk or chocolate milk have to be ice cold.

Lunch

Dinner

Study Guide

Subject _____
Pages _____ to _____
Unit/Chapter Title _____

Main Idea_____
1. _____
  _____
2. _____
  _____
3. _____
  _____
4. _____
  _____
5. _____
  _____
6. _____
  _____

Keepin' It Simple!
Writing simple sentences, identifying main ideas

Pull out a science or social studies text for a sentence-writing activity that serves double duty! Guide each student to set up a study guide similar to the one shown for a current chapter or unit of study. Next, direct the child to read a chapter or selection from his text. After he reads, guide him to write a simple sentence that states the main idea of each paragraph or section. When he's finished, he'll not only have practiced writing meaningful simple sentences and identified main ideas, but he'll have prepared a great study guide to boot!

Compound Collaboration
Combining simple sentences to write compound sentences

Students will be clamoring to write compound sentences with this fun game! Have each child write five simple sentences on lined paper—skipping a line between each sentence—and then cut the sentences into strips. Review with the class that compound sentences include at least two simple sentences that are connected by a comma and a conjunction or by a semicolon. Next, divide students into groups of four. Explain that each child will have ten minutes to combine her group's simple sentences and write as many compound sentences on a sheet of paper as she can. Instruct each student to place her strips faceup in the center of the group and begin writing compound sentences at your signal. When the time is up, have group members trade papers and tally the number of correct compound sentences on each paper. The player with the highest number in each group wins! To play another round, each child retrieves her strips and works with a different group of classmates.

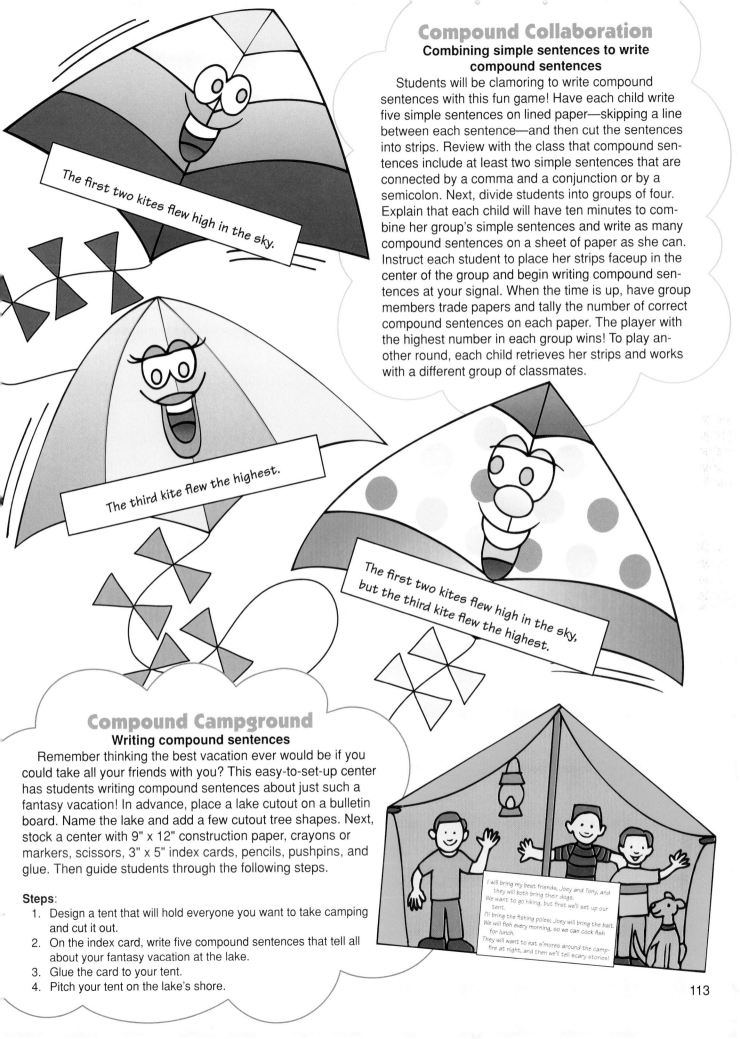

The first two kites flew high in the sky.

The third kite flew the highest.

The first two kites flew high in the sky, but the third kite flew the highest.

Compound Campground
Writing compound sentences

Remember thinking the best vacation ever would be if you could take all your friends with you? This easy-to-set-up center has students writing compound sentences about just such a fantasy vacation! In advance, place a lake cutout on a bulletin board. Name the lake and add a few cutout tree shapes. Next, stock a center with 9" x 12" construction paper, crayons or markers, scissors, 3" x 5" index cards, pencils, pushpins, and glue. Then guide students through the following steps.

Steps:
1. Design a tent that will hold everyone you want to take camping and cut it out.
2. On the index card, write five compound sentences that tell all about your fantasy vacation at the lake.
3. Glue the card to your tent.
4. Pitch your tent on the lake's shore.

I will bring my best friends, Joey and Tony, and they will both bring their dogs.
We want to go hiking, but first we'll set up our tent.
I'll bring the fishing poles; Joey will bring the bait.
We will fish every morning, so we can cook fish for lunch.
They will want to eat s'mores around the campfire at night, and then we'll tell scary stories!

113

Complex Sentences Made Simple

Writing complex sentences

Liven up the writing of complex sentences with this creative auditory exercise. First, review with students that a complex sentence is made up of one independent clause and at least one dependent clause. Next, write on the board the complex sentence template shown. Then direct each student to use the template to write ten different complex sentences. Allow time for each student to share his favorite sentence with the class and accompany it with the matching sound effect!

When _____, it sounds like _____.

When Dad does the dishes, it sounds like he's playing the cymbals. Crash! Crash! Clink!

My cat, Tabby, likes to stay outside. because she likes to hunt.

Get to the Point!

Using complex sentences to enhance or clarify meaning

Show students that adding dependent clauses can create complex sentences that really get to the point! In advance, copy the sentences below on the board. Then pair students and give each twosome ten 1" x 4½" strips of construction paper, scissors, and glue. Have the partners cut one end of each strip into a point. Next, instruct each duo to copy the first sentence on the board onto a sheet of lined paper. Then direct the partners to write on a strip a dependent clause that will enhance or clarify the sentence and glue the strip in place as shown. Have pairs repeat the process with each remaining sentence. Now that's getting to the point!

1. My cat, Tabby, likes to stay outside.
2. Fergus chased Tabby into the woods.
3. There used to be more trees in the woods.
4. Did you see the new park?
5. Some of the equipment is missing.
6. Let's go to the park.
7. My cousin might come too.
8. Tabby hasn't come home.
9. We can look for Tabby.
10. We'll find Tabby.

Whose Note Is It?

Simple Sid always uses simple sentences.
Compound Carla always uses compound sentences.
Complex Conrad always uses complex sentences.

Kathy Kite's kids left notes for her, but they forgot to sign them! To help her sort the notes, label each kite shape below with the correct child's name.

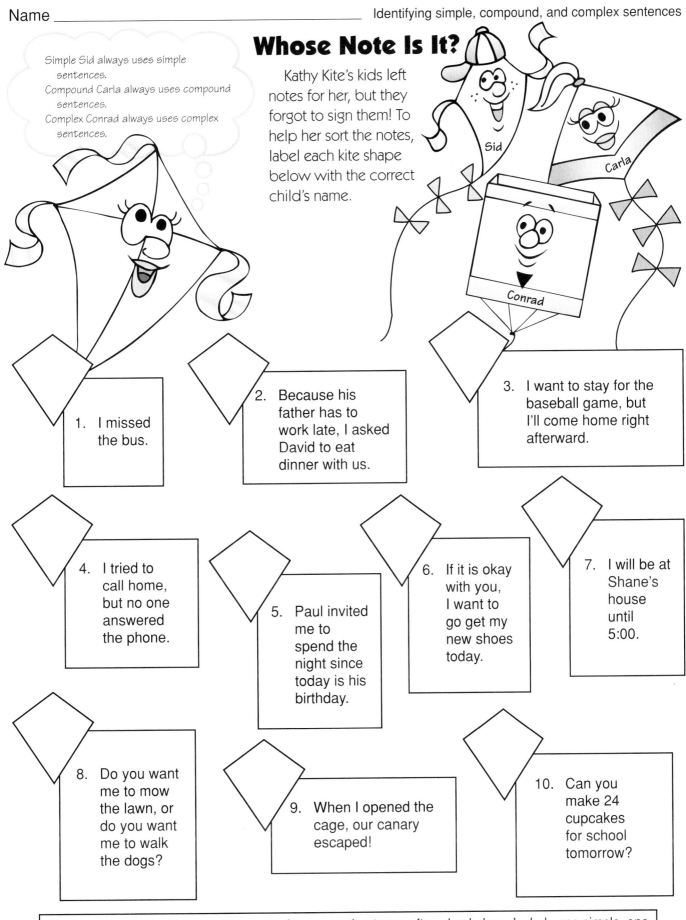

Sid

Carla

Conrad

1. I missed the bus.

2. Because his father has to work late, I asked David to eat dinner with us.

3. I want to stay for the baseball game, but I'll come home right afterward.

4. I tried to call home, but no one answered the phone.

5. Paul invited me to spend the night since today is his birthday.

6. If it is okay with you, I want to go get my new shoes today.

7. I will be at Shane's house until 5:00.

8. Do you want me to mow the lawn, or do you want me to walk the dogs?

9. When I opened the cage, our canary escaped!

10. Can you make 24 cupcakes for school tomorrow?

Bonus Box: On the back of this page, write a note about your afterschool plans. Include one simple, one compound, and one complex sentence.

Reading Fluency: The

Getting students front-row seats at this award-winning show is sure to increase their reading fluency!

Kim Minafo, Dillard Drive Elementary School, Raleigh, NC

Clearly Fluent Readers
Developing fluency with reading tools

Is there a simple tool that can help your students become more fluent readers? You bet! Give each student a clear overhead transparency, a wipe-off marker, two paper clips, and a copy of a short reading passage. Direct him to paper-clip his transparency atop the passage as shown. Next, have him skim the passage and use the wipe-off marker to underline any unfamiliar words. When he is finished, instruct him to discuss with a partner the pronunciations and meanings of the underlined words. Then have him read his passage again, this time placing marks to show where pauses or breaks in the text are appropriate. After he reads through the passage several more times to establish fluency and make any additional adjustments, have him share his markings with his partner. Once he cleans his transparency, it's ready to store for future use!

Bravo!

Once upon a time...

PLAYBILL

Homework
Oh, homework, why do you take so long?
Don't you know I want to play?
Oh, homework, I don't think you belong
On such a wonderful day.

Line-by-Line Fluency
Using poetry to practice fluency

With a poem in your pocket, you can teach fluency without missing a beat! Make two copies of the same entertaining poem for each pair of students. Direct the partners to cut apart one copy of the poem line by line and then place both the cut and uncut copies in a resealable bag. Next, read the poem aloud to the class. Also discuss with students the importance of rhythm and help them determine the poem's beat. Then instruct each duo to read the uncut copy of the poem aloud to each other and use it as a guide to arrange the cut pieces in the correct order. When they are finished, have one student pick up the poem's first line and read it aloud while his partner softly counts the beats. Then have the second student pick up the poem's second line and read it aloud while the first partner softly counts the beats. Once the pairs have practiced reading the entire poem with the correct rhythm, guide the whole class to read the poem together and clap to the beat. It's as easy as 1, 2, 3!

Hottest Ticket in Town!

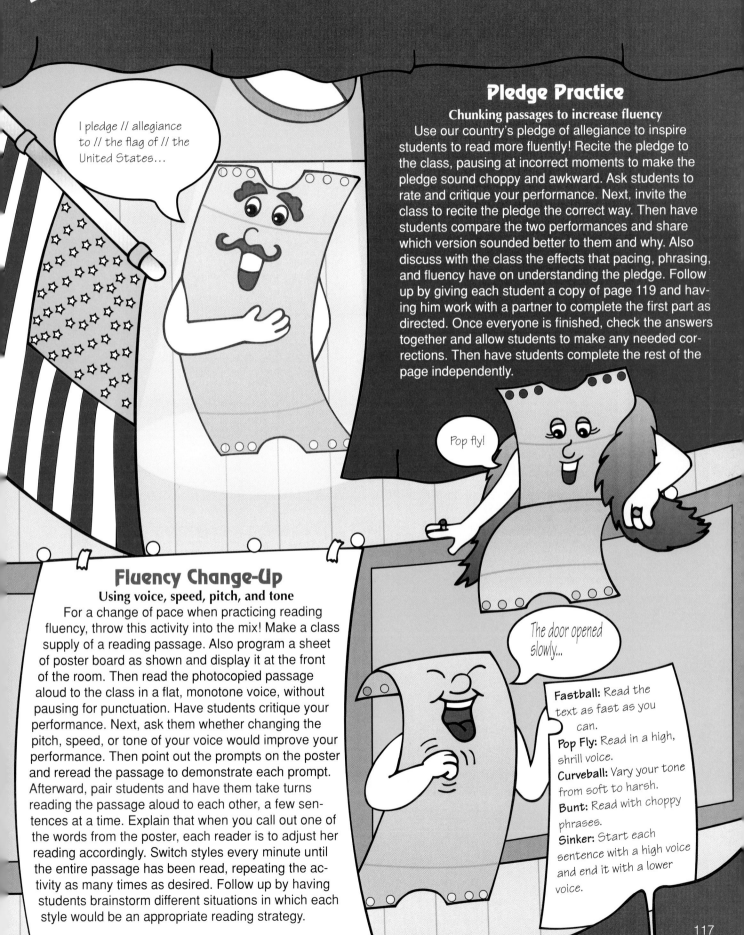

I pledge // allegiance to // the flag of // the United States...

Pledge Practice
Chunking passages to increase fluency

Use our country's pledge of allegiance to inspire students to read more fluently! Recite the pledge to the class, pausing at incorrect moments to make the pledge sound choppy and awkward. Ask students to rate and critique your performance. Next, invite the class to recite the pledge the correct way. Then have students compare the two performances and share which version sounded better to them and why. Also discuss with the class the effects that pacing, phrasing, and fluency have on understanding the pledge. Follow up by giving each student a copy of page 119 and having him work with a partner to complete the first part as directed. Once everyone is finished, check the answers together and allow students to make any needed corrections. Then have students complete the rest of the page independently.

Pop fly!

The door opened slowly...

Fluency Change-Up
Using voice, speed, pitch, and tone

For a change of pace when practicing reading fluency, throw this activity into the mix! Make a class supply of a reading passage. Also program a sheet of poster board as shown and display it at the front of the room. Then read the photocopied passage aloud to the class in a flat, monotone voice, without pausing for punctuation. Have students critique your performance. Next, ask them whether changing the pitch, speed, or tone of your voice would improve your performance. Then point out the prompts on the poster and reread the passage to demonstrate each prompt. Afterward, pair students and have them take turns reading the passage aloud to each other, a few sentences at a time. Explain that when you call out one of the words from the poster, each reader is to adjust her reading accordingly. Switch styles every minute until the entire passage has been read, repeating the activity as many times as desired. Follow up by having students brainstorm different situations in which each style would be an appropriate reading strategy.

Fastball: Read the text as fast as you can.
Pop Fly: Read in a high, shrill voice.
Curveball: Vary your tone from soft to harsh.
Bunt: Read with choppy phrases.
Sinker: Start each sentence with a high voice and end it with a lower voice.

Class List
- Marius
- Fantasia
- Marty
- Annie
- Gina
- Laurie
- Meg
- Maria
- Dolly
- Hunt

Maria,
I really enjoyed...

HeeHee   HoHo

Laugh-Out-Loud Practice

Practicing pacing, intonation, and expression

Students will be eager to practice fluency skills if you use laugh-out-loud limericks! Ask your librarian to gather limerick books for your class. Then select a limerick to read aloud to the class. Discuss with students the limerick's rhyming pattern *(aabba)* and the rhythm and speed at which to read it. Next, have each child choose a limerick from a book, or invite her to write an original limerick of her own. Then divide students into groups and have each group practice reading its limericks aloud, focusing on fluency, tone, and expression. Finally, have each group member read her limerick aloud while the rest of the group taps to the beat. Once students are comfortable performing their limericks, send the groups to a neighboring classroom to show off their skills! For more practice, have each child complete a copy of page 120 as directed.

HarHar   HaHa

Rainbow Reading Assessment

Assessing oral reading

Here's a colorful tip to help you manage oral-reading assessments! On your class roster, randomly color-code students into groups of four or five. Each day, pick a different color group to evaluate. Begin by reading aloud from any student text; then pause and call, "Time out!" Explain that when students hear this prompt, each child should pick up reading where you stopped, reading aloud in a quiet voice that can only be heard by the person closest to her. While students are reading softly to their partners, move around the room, listening to individual readers from the selected color group. As you do so, write a brief progress note for each child's records or an encouraging note to place on her desk. After a few minutes say, "Time in!" to signal students to stop reading aloud so the lesson can continue as before. Assessing oral reading has never been so simple!

There once was a tailless dog in my yard
Who liked to dig holes and play cards.
But one day he set sail
In search of his tail,
And, boy, did I take it hard!

Chunking sentences to improve fluency

Marks of Fluency

Stella found some poems about famous American symbols. But she needs your help to read them. Use a colored pencil to divide each poem into phrases that make it easier to read and understand.

1. These men are carved in stone high above the fruited plain, and visitors come to see them from California to Maine.

2. Sweet bell of freedom, now old and worn, you cracked just as our nation was born. Years after repair, you cracked again. How you are now is how you'll remain.

3. Just beside the harbor's door stands a statue tall and sure. She welcomes the tired, the weak, and the poor. She lights the way to our country's shore.

4. A declaration told the king that freedom waited in the wings. It told him why and made it clear that England's flag would not fly here.

What famous American symbol is each poem above about?

1. _____

2. _____

3. _____

4. _____

Bonus Box: On the back of this page, write your own poem about a famous American symbol. Then practice reading it aloud to a friend.

The Best of The Mailbox® • *Grades 4–6* • ©The Mailbox® Books • TEC61169 • Key p. 188

Note to the teacher: Use with "Pledge Practice" on page 117. Each student will need a colored pencil to complete this page.

Performing Lloyd's Laugh Lines

The big show is only days away, and Lloyd is having trouble with his
lines! His friend Larry is helping him practice so he'll get lots of laughs.

Help Larry divide the rest of Lloyd's lines correctly. Then practice reading them aloud with a partner.

1 | My younger brother wanted a pet. He said he'd take anything that he could get. But when I brought him a snake, the kid started to quake and fell to the ground in a sweat!

2 | Consider yourself quite a fan? Let me tell you about my neighbor, Dan. He went opening day and decided to stay. Four months later, he's still in the stands!

3 | Mrs. Wilson just visited Mars. She brought us all back candy bars that are made by wee folk who sell eggs with six yolks and carry their children in jars!

4 | I once knew a man who had eyes that got larger each time he told lies. They started off small, but in no time at all, they'd grown to 50 times the normal size!

5 | My sister plays music each spring. She's loud and she makes my ears ring. She's a rock and roll star, and I'm sure she'll go far, so long as she learns how to sing!

The Best of The Mailbox® • *Grades 4–6* • ©The Mailbox® Books • TEC61169 • Key p. 189

LITERATURE RESPONSE UNITS

Examining Characters
Analyzing Characters in Literature

Take a closer look at the characters your students read about with the following literary analysis activities.

with ideas by Marcia Barton, Prairieville, LA

Baggage Check

Analyzing a character's traits, critical thinking

If you're ready to send weak literary analysis skills packing, then this hands-on activity should do the trick! After reading a story or book, divide the class into pairs. Have each pair use the materials and steps shown to create a suitcase that's packed with a favorite character's traits. Post the completed bags on a bulletin board; then challenge students to look at the traits inside each suitcase and guess the identity of the character who packed it.

Materials for each student pair: file folder, scissors, 12" x 18" sheet of brown construction paper, glue, used magazines, marker, unlined index card, tape, 4" length of yarn

Steps:
1. Trim a file folder as shown to make a suitcase shape.
2. Glue the opened suitcase shape on the brown construction paper. Cut around the suitcase to leave a small border of brown as shown. Let the glue dry.
3. Crease the suitcase at the fold. Cut a handle from the brown paper scraps and glue it to the suitcase as shown.
4. Choose a character from the story. Brainstorm at least five traits this character displays.
5. For each trait, cut out a magazine picture that illustrates or represents that quality. (For example, a mirror could represent a character's self-centeredness.)
6. Glue each picture inside the suitcase and label it with the matching trait.
7. Fold the index card in half to make a luggage tag. Write "Who Am I?" on the front of the tag. Write the character's name on the inside.
8. Tape the tag to one end of the yarn. Tie the other end around the suitcase's handle.

Plus and Minus

Analyzing a character's traits

Use this idea to encourage students to search for both the good and not-so-good traits exhibited by a story's characters. After reading aloud the first chapter (or more) of a novel, list with students the characters encountered. On the board, draw a chart such as the one shown and label it with a character's name. Then invite students to name positive and negative traits that the character displayed as you list them on the board. Have students include the page number where the trait is described or evident.

Next, give each student an eight-inch circle of pastel construction paper. Have him fold his circle in half, open it, and draw a chart like the one on the board. Then direct the student to select one character (other than the one discussed earlier) and fill in the chart as he continues reading the book. To keep track of his chart, have the student fold the circle in half and use it as a bookmark. After students have read for several days (or have finished the book), extend this activity with "Flat or Round?" on page 123.

122

Flat or Round?

Identifying flat and round characters

Introduce the literary concept of flat and round characters with this follow-up to the "Plus and Minus" activity on page 122. A *round character* is well-developed, displays both positive and negative qualities, and undergoes change during the story. Like a cardboard cutout, a *flat character* lacks complexity and will not change or develop during the story. After students share the bookmarks they made in "Plus and Minus," discuss these questions:

- Which kind of character—flat or round—is most like a real person?
- Which famous characters in cartoons, movies, and television are flat? Which are round? Explain your choices.
- Which type makes the best main character? Why?
- Why might an author include flat characters in a story?
- How would you categorize the character you charted on your bookmark? Why?

Warning: Conflict Ahead!

Analyzing a character's conflicts, recalling story events

A good story always includes a conflict or two (or more!). Try this activity to help students analyze how characters confront and overcome obstacles. After the class finishes a story or book, divide students into groups. Have each group use the materials and steps shown to create a poster that illustrates the conflicts faced by a favorite character.

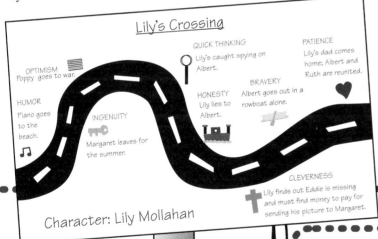

Materials for each group: sheet of poster board, markers or crayons, scissors, glue, construction paper scraps

Steps:

1. Choose a character. Brainstorm a list of the character's traits.
2. List the obstacles that your character encounters during the story. Write the conflicts in the order in which they occur, ending with the story's conclusion.
3. Make a small symbol from construction paper to represent each obstacle.
4. On the poster board, draw and color a road. Glue the obstacles in order along the road. Label each obstacle.
5. Write the character's name and the title of your book or story on the poster.
6. Decide as a group which trait(s) listed in Step 1 the character used to overcome each obstacle. Write the trait beside the obstacle.
7. Share your poster with the class.

What If...?

Analyzing the effect of a character's traits on the plot

What would have happened in *Charlotte's Web* if trusting Wilbur hadn't believed his spider friend when she said she liked him? What if Aunt Spiker and Aunt Sponge had not been horrible toward James in *James and the Giant Peach*? Challenge students to think about how a character's traits affect the plot of a story with this simple activity. With the class, choose a character and brainstorm a list of his or her character traits. Next, assign one trait to each student. Direct the student to use a thesaurus to find one or more antonyms for the trait. Then have the student write a paragraph that tells how the book (or chapter) would have ended differently if the character had displayed the opposite trait instead of the actual one. Provide time for students to share their paragraphs with the class.

Closer Than They Appear

Identifying a foil, writing poetry

Sometimes an author will include a foil in his or her story. A *foil* is a character who sharply contrasts with the protagonist. The author includes the foil as a way to highlight traits of the main character. For example, a foil might be extremely greedy to highlight the generosity of the main character.

If the novel your class is reading includes a foil, try this activity. First, enlarge the rearview mirror pattern, shown below, on construction paper for each pair of students. Divide the class into pairs. Then have each twosome brainstorm ways that the foil's traits and actions call attention to those of the main character. After students share their lists, have each pair use the materials and steps shown to create a diamante poem that shows the differences between the two characters. Discuss Step 5 and why this message found on many rearview mirrors is appropriate when comparing a protagonist and a foil. *(There's a closer relationship between the main character and the foil than might appear at first.)* Post the poems on a bulletin board titled "Closer Than They Appear."

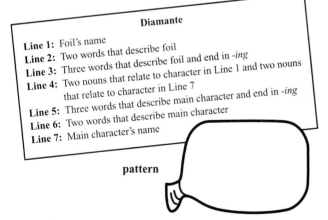

Diamante

Line 1: Foil's name
Line 2: Two words that describe foil
Line 3: Three words that describe foil and end in *-ing*
Line 4: Two nouns that relate to character in Line 1 and two nouns that relate to character in Line 7
Line 5: Three words that describe main character and end in *-ing*
Line 6: Two words that describe main character
Line 7: Main character's name

pattern

The Best of The Mailbox® • Grades 4–6 • ©The Mailbox® Books • TEC61169

Materials for each student pair: mirror pattern, 8" strip of aluminum foil, scissors, fine-point permanent marker, glue

Steps:
1. Use the form above to write a diamante about the book's main character and foil.
2. Cut a piece of aluminum foil to fit inside the mirror pattern.
3. Use the marker to copy the poem onto the aluminum foil.
4. Glue the aluminum foil on the pattern as shown.
5. Write the following along the bottom of the aluminum foil: "OBJECTS IN MIRROR ARE CLOSER THAN THEY APPEAR."

Things Have Gotta Change!

Identifying static and changing characters, writing an explanation

Help students understand how characters change (or don't change) with this group activity. First, explain that a *static character* basically stays the same throughout the story. *Changing characters* change during the story because of what happens to them. Ask students to name characters the class has read about; then have them categorize each character as static or changing, providing evidence to support each choice.

Next, divide the class into small groups. Assign each group a character from the book students have just completed. Have each group use an overhead projector to trace two large silhouettes on white paper to represent its character. Then have the group follow these steps:

1. Cut out the silhouettes. Place them on a table facing each other.
2. Label the tracing on the left "BEFORE" and the one on the right "AFTER."
3. On the "BEFORE" silhouette, use colored pencils or markers to list traits the character displayed at the beginning of the story. On the "AFTER" shape, list traits exhibited at the end.
4. Glue the silhouettes on a large sheet of construction paper as shown. Write the character's name on the poster.

After the groups have shared their posters, have each student write a paragraph explaining the events and circumstances that caused his assigned character to change. Display these paragraphs with the posters.

Inside Private Eye

A good author doesn't just tell a reader what a character looks like on the outside. A good author also gives the reader information about what the character is like on the inside.

Part I:

1. Fill out the ID card for one character from your book. Draw a picture in the photo box.
2. Pretend that you are the character. On each line below, write one phrase about yourself.

Name _____

Age _____

Gender _____

Distinguishing physical traits:

_____

_____

_____

_____

Photo

I like

- _____
- _____
- _____
- _____
- _____
- _____

I don't like

- _____
- _____
- _____
- _____
- _____
- _____

I believe

- _____
- _____
- _____
- _____
- _____
- _____

I dream

- _____
- _____
- _____
- _____
- _____
- _____

Part II: Continue pretending that you are the character you selected. Write one event from the book on these lines. _____

_____

On your own paper, write a letter to another character in the story. Use some of the phrases listed above to explain why you responded the way you did in that situation.

Bonus Box: On the back of this page, write three phrases about yourself for each of the four boxes above. Then use the phrases to write a paragraph titled "This Is Who I Am."

Bravo to Books From Different Genres!

Helping Students Recognize and Read Different Genres

Want to help your students learn the special features of different genres? Eager for them to read a variety of texts? Then you're sure to applaud the following repertoire of literary analysis activities!

with ideas by Judy Haun, Maryville, TN

Group Genre Posters
Identifying characteristics of different genres, comparing and contrasting genres

Familiarize your students with the characteristics of different genres with a group activity that's "do-re-magnificent"!

Part 1: Write the name of each genre listed at the right on a separate slip of paper. Place the slips in a paper bag. Review the information shown with students. Then divide the class into small groups and give each group a sheet of poster board and markers, crayons, or colored pencils. Have one member from each group draw a slip from the bag. Then have the group label the top half of its poster with the name of the selected genre, its characteristics, and an example of a book from that genre. On the sides of the poster, have the group add illustrations that will help others remember the genre's features. Tape the finished posters on your classroom's walls.

Part 2: Brainstorm with students a list of books the class has read. After students identify each book's genre, write each title on the appropriate poster. Then have each student label a self-sticking note with the title of the book he's currently reading and stick it on the appropriate poster as shown. Discuss with students reasons why some posters have more notes than others. Ask questions such as the following: Why do you seem to prefer certain genres over others? How are the genres similar? How are they different? What is the benefit of reading books from a variety of genres? After the discussion, place a pad of self-sticking notes on a table or shelf. Then encourage students to add new titles to the posters as they read. For a related activity, see the reproducible on page 128.

Genres

autobiography: story an author writes about his or her own life

biography: writer's story about someone else's life

drama: fiction that is meant to be performed for an audience, also known as a play

fable: short story that teaches a moral or lesson and often features talking animals

fairy tale: folktale featuring magic and supernatural elements that conveys a lesson of morality

fantasy: story that takes place in a make-believe setting, usually features characters with magical or supernatural powers

folktale: story originally passed on by word of mouth from one generation of a community to another, usually less serious than a myth

historical fiction: fiction story that is mixed with facts and is based on a real place and time in history

legend: folk story set in the present or the past and based on real events and people

mystery: story that usually features characters who try to solve a crime

myth: traditional story written to explain a people's beliefs, a natural event, or the relationships of humans beings and gods, goddesses, and heroes

nonfiction: writing that is factual rather than fictional

poetry: writing that is usually in verse and uses brief, colorful, and often rhythmic language to express human emotions and thoughts

realistic fiction: story with imaginary characters and events that could exist in the real world

science fiction: story that is based on new or futuristic scientific developments

tall tale: humorous story that features superhuman accomplishments and may be based on a real person's life

You Blow My Doors Off!
Reading texts from a variety of genres, writing a book review

Use an easy-to-make display to challenge students to read books from a variety of different genres. First, decorate four sheets of construction paper to resemble doors as shown. Label each door with the name of a genre your students typically don't choose to read. Then staple each door along its left side to a bulletin board, creasing it so that it opens as shown. Finally, staple a sheet of lined paper behind each door. Add the title "Can You Blow My Doors Off?" to the display.

After the display is completed, challenge students to read books from the genres listed on the doors. When a student finishes a book, have him write a brief book review and share it with the class. Then have him write his book's title and author on the lined paper behind the appropriate door. When ten books are listed behind a door, announce, "You've blown my door off!" Then remove the door and list of books from the display. (Post the list near your classroom library as a source of reading recommendations.) When students have blown off all the doors, celebrate by watching the video version of a favorite book and munching on popcorn. Then post four new doors and repeat the challenge using different genres.

Genre Card File
Reading a variety of texts, writing a book summary

Keep track of your students' independent reading while you nudge them to read a greater variety of texts. How? With this simple management tip! All you need is a supply of white and colored index cards and an inexpensive recipe card box with numbered dividers (one per student plus one extra). Store the cards behind the last divider. Inside the box's lid, glue a color code such as the one shown. Finally, assign a number to each student.

When a student reads a book independently, she pulls an appropriately colored card from the back of the box and labels it with the information shown. Then she files the card behind her numbered divider. Watching their individual collections of cards grow is sure to motivate your students. Plus, seeing only a few colors of cards will alert both you and the student that she needs to branch out and try a new genre.
Linda Landes, Camden Elementary, Camden, IN

127

Help Me, Marian!

The six people below have just been issued new library cards. Each person has told Marian the Librarian about his or her interests. Now Marian wants to make suggestions about genres each reader would enjoy.

Directions: Read the description of each reader. Then, on the library card's lines, write the genres from the box that the person would probably be most interested in reading. On the back of this page, list your reasons for each genre choice.

1. Ima Reeder
Ima loves reading about the lives of famous people. Her favorite book is about Harriet Tubman. Ima, who loves to mountain climb, also enjoys reading books about the world's tallest mountains.

_____   _____

2. Booker Mark
Booker likes drawing pictures about imaginary lands and magical creatures. He also can't get enough of stories that feature gods, goddesses, and heroes.

_____   _____

3. Paige Turner
When Paige isn't reading, you can find her on a stage rehearsing a play. Her favorite TV show is *Crime Solvers, Inc.* Paige's favorite book is *George Washington and the Cherry Tree.*

_____   _____

4. Telmia Story
As a child, Telmia adored Mother Goose rhymes. She often expresses her emotions and thoughts in verse. Telmia likes imaginary stories with believable characters and events.

_____   _____

5. Kant Putitdown
Kant loves reading stories that teach lessons about how to live life and treat others kindly. He also likes to hear his grandparents tell stories about his family's history.

_____   _____

6. Reid Wunmorchapter
Reid can often be found daydreaming about the future. He also likes to read stories that are based on real places and times in history.

_____   _____

GENRES

autobiography	fable	historical fiction	mystery	poetry
biography	fantasy	legend	myth	realistic fiction
drama	folktale		nonfiction	science fiction

Bonus Box: On the back of this page, write what your library card would say if it included a few sentences about your interests.

The Best of The Mailbox® • Grades 4–6 • ©The Mailbox® Books • TEC61169 • Key p. 189

128 **Note to the teacher:** Use alone or with "Group Genre Posters" on page 126.

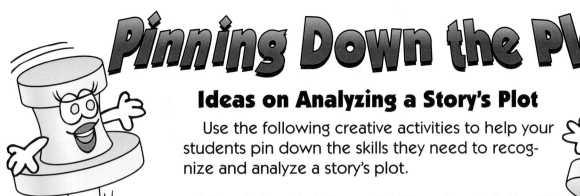

Pinning Down the Plot

Ideas on Analyzing a Story's Plot

Use the following creative activities to help your students pin down the skills they need to recognize and analyze a story's plot.

with ideas by Terry Healy, Eugene Field Elementary, Manhattan, KS

Once Upon a Plot
Identifying the parts of a plot

Once upon a time, there was an activity that introduced students to the parts of a plot—and here it is! In advance, label chart paper with the information about plot parts on page 131. Also ask your librarian for five or six picture books that retell familiar fairy tales. Next, ask a student to retell *The Three Little Pigs*. Explain that this fairy tale, like any story, has a *plot,* or the events that take place in a story. Display the information from page 131 and discuss it with students. Then divide the class into groups and give each group chart paper and a marker. Direct each group to list the five parts of a plot down the left side of the paper. Then have the group identify and list the plot parts of *The Three Little Pigs* (see the sample chart). Provide time for groups to share and compare their charts. Then give each group a fairy-tale picture book and a new sheet of chart paper. Challenge the group to read its book and complete a second chart analyzing the story's plot. Follow up by having students complete the reproducible activity on page 131.

Plot Analysis of
The Three Little Pigs

Exposition: The three pigs and the hungry wolf are introduced.

Rising action: The wolf blows down the first two pigs' houses.

Climax: The wolf falls down the chimney of the third pig's house and lands in the cooking pot.

Falling action: The pigs realize they are safe. They decide to live together in the third pig's house.

Resolution: The pigs live happily ever after.

Harry finds out he's a wizard.

Hagrid

PLOT POWER POINTS

Plot Power Play
Identifying parts of a plot

Follow up the reading of any story or class read-aloud with a game that puts the parts of a plot in their place! List the five parts of a plot (see page 131) on the board. Then give each student two paper slips. Direct the student to label each slip with a different event or character from the story. Collect the strips in a container, adding three more strips labeled "Plot Power Points." Then divide the class into two teams and guide students through the playing rules below.

To play:
1. The first player from Team A draws a slip and follows these directions:
   - If the strip is labeled with an event, identify the part of the plot in which it happened.
   - If the slip is labeled with a character, identify the plot part in which the character is introduced.
   - If the slip is labeled "Plot Power Points," add two points to your team's score.
2. Discuss Player 1's answer. Award one point to his team if it is correct.
3. Repeat Steps 1–2 with the first player from Team B.
4. Continue play until time is up or all the slips have been drawn. Declare the team with more points the winner.

Cause-and-Effect Chains
Understanding how cause-and-effect relationships affect a plot's development

To demonstrate for students how cause-and-effect relationships affect a plot's development, list on the board the story starters shown. Then divide the class into six groups. Number the groups 1–6. Then give each group tape and seven same-colored index cards (making sure each group receives a different color). Guide students through these steps:

1. Choose a story starter and write it on an index card.
2. Predict a result, or effect, of the action listed on the card. Write this effect on a second card. Then tape the second card to the right side of the first card as shown.
3. Pass your chain of cards to the next group.
4. Read the events listed on your two new cards. Then repeat Steps 2–3.
5. Continue in this manner until your original chain has been returned to your group.

At the end of the activity, collect the groups' chains. Then read aloud each chain and discuss how the cause-and-effect relationships listed on it affect the plot of the resulting story. If desired, give each group a chain other than its own. Then challenge students (individually or as a group) to write a story based on their group's chain.

Story Starters
- Gina hit a ball.
- Jamal overslept.
- Tony saved $50.00.
- Mark bumped into Elyse.
- Cami phoned Kelsey.
- Rebecca was late.
- Noah caught a cold.

Jamal overslept.	He missed the bus for the championship game.	He called his grandfather to give him a ride.

Pass the Plot Pops, Please!
Identifying the parts of a plot, completing a book report

Turn your next book report project into a unique exercise on identifying the parts of a plot. Have each student bring an empty food box (cereal, cake mix, pasta, etc.) to school. Give each child four sheets of white construction paper; scissors; glue; and markers, crayons, or colored pencils. Then have her follow these steps to create a cool book-on-a-box project.

1. Cut off the top flaps of the box.
2. On scrap paper, draw a rough draft to show how you will label and illustrate the front, back, and sides of your box with the following information:
   - Front of box: name of product; exposition; book's title, author, and genre; your name
   - Back of box: rising action and climax, picture of free prize (related to the plot) that's inside the box
   - Side panel 1: falling action and resolution
   - Side panel 2: brief review of the book
3. Cover the front, back, and sides of the box with white construction paper.
4. Label and illustrate the box according to the rough draft you completed in Step 2.
5. Inside the box, place a drawing that illustrates the story's climax.

??? My Review

Mysterious Plot Pops

Breakfast of Super-sleuths

Running out of Time by Margaret Peterson Haddix

Jessie and her family live in Clifton in 1840— or do they?

It's a mystery to me!

Natalie

Pinning Down the Plot

What's the most important part of a story to pin down? The plot! The *plot* is all of the events that take place in a story from its beginning to the end. A plot has five parts: exposition, rising action, climax, falling action, and resolution.

Directions: Think about a story you have just read. In the notes shown, summarize each part of the story's plot. Use the definition on each note to help you. Color each pushpin after you complete that note.

Exposition
First part of the story in which the characters, setting, and conflict are introduced

_____
_____
_____
_____
_____

Rising Action
Part of the story in which the main character tries to solve his or her problem

_____
_____
_____
_____
_____

Climax
Most important or exciting part of the story

_____
_____
_____
_____
_____

Falling Action
Part of the story in which the main character begins learning how to face life after the problem has been solved, possibly gaining valuable insights

_____
_____
_____
_____
_____

Resolution
Part of the plot that brings the story to a close

_____
_____
_____
_____
_____

Note to the teacher: Use with "Once Upon a Plot" on page 129 or alone. Each student will need a crayon, marker, or colored pencil to complete the page. If desired, also use this graphic organizer to help a student develop the plot of an original story he wants to write.

Rip-Roarin' Responses to Literature

Give your students some "grrreat" ways to respond to literature with the following creative ideas!

with ideas by Kim Minafo, Cary, NC

Response Quilt

Need to help students warm up to the idea of responding to literature? Then cozy up to the reproducible **booklet** on page 134! To begin, have each student fold a sheet of white copy paper into six sections as shown below. Instruct the child to unfold his paper, cut apart the six boxes, and staple them together at the top. Then have him use a small piece of Sticky-Tac to mount the resulting booklet on his copy of page 134 where indicated. Next, guide students through the steps shown. When everyone is finished, discuss why students chose the prompts they did and talk about their responses. Then have each child remove his booklet so he can replace it with a new one when you want to repeat the activity.

Steps:
1. Label the first page of your booklet with the reading assignment. Then read the selection.
2. Choose a prompt from a quilt square on page 134. Write your response on the second page of the booklet. Then draw on the page the symbol from the matching quilt square.
3. Repeat Step 2 for each of the remaining pages, using a different prompt on each page.

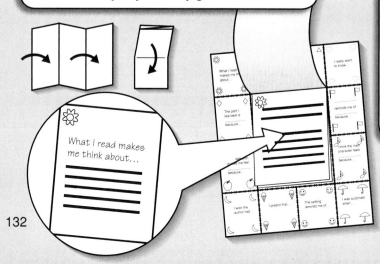

Colorful Support

"Hues" this colorful **partner** idea to help students respond thoughtfully to what they read. After students have read a passage, divide the class into pairs. Give each twosome ten small self-sticking notes, five each of two different colors. Then write two of the questions shown on the board, labeling each with a note's color. Next, direct each pair to discuss the questions. After the discussion, have each pair use the notes of one color to identify the parts of the text that support their responses to that question. Have them use the other set of notes to mark text references that helped them respond to the other question. When all groups are ready, discuss the students' responses as a class.

Questions
- What words did the author use to catch your attention?
- What new information did you learn?
- What do you think is the main idea of this section?
- What parts left you with questions?
- What parts did you find difficult to understand?
- What do you think will happen next?
- Which character interests you the most?
- What mood do you think the author is trying to create?

| YELLOW | What mood do you think the author is trying to create? | |
| BLUE | What new information did you learn? | |

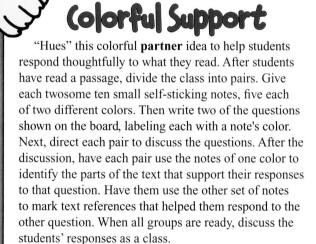

132

All-Star Responses

For a **whole-group** literature response activity that can be used year-round, try this all-star idea! Cut five stars each from red, blue, and yellow construction paper. Glue one star of each color to the outside of a brown paper lunch bag. Place the remaining stars in the bag. Then display a copy of the questions chart shown.

After all students have read a selection, have one child pull a star from the bag. Direct him to choose a matching question from the chart and respond to it. Encourage other students to build on his response. Then have another child draw a star from the bag and repeat the activity. Collect the stars at the end of the activity. Pull out the bag again the next time you're looking for some all-star literature responses!

Fiction Questions	
Red:	What do you think about the main character?
	What other character do you think is interesting? Why?
Blue:	Did the author help you visualize the setting? How?
	Was the setting believable? Why or why not?
	Could the story have taken place somewhere else? Why or why not?
Yellow:	What surprised you about what happened in this section?
	What was most believable?
	What do you think will happen next?

Nonfiction Questions	
Red:	How did this passage build on what you already know?
Blue:	Was this passage easy to understand? Why or why not?
	How did the author help you understand the ideas?
	What new information did you learn?
Yellow:	What questions do you have?
	What information was difficult for you to understand?
	What information, if any, might you research next?

A "Pizza" the Pie

Serve up a fun way to respond to a **nonfiction text** using this cool group activity. After students have read a nonfiction selection, divide the class into groups of six. Give each group glue, an eight-inch circle cut from beige paper, and a seven-inch red paper circle that's been cut into six slices as shown. Then follow these steps:

1. Instruct each group to discuss the selection and then write the main idea along the edge of the beige circle.
2. Direct each group member to take a red paper slice. Have each student label the top half of his slice with a sentence about background knowledge or personal experience that helped him understand the passage.
3. Have each student label the bottom half of his slice with a sentence about the new information he learned from the passage.
4. Direct each group member to share his slice with the group. Then have students take turns gluing the slices to the crust circle to create a pizza.

Discuss with students how both components on the slices helped them understand the selection's main idea. Then display the pizzas on a bulletin board.

Warming Up to Literature

Complete this cozy quilt by following your teacher's directions.

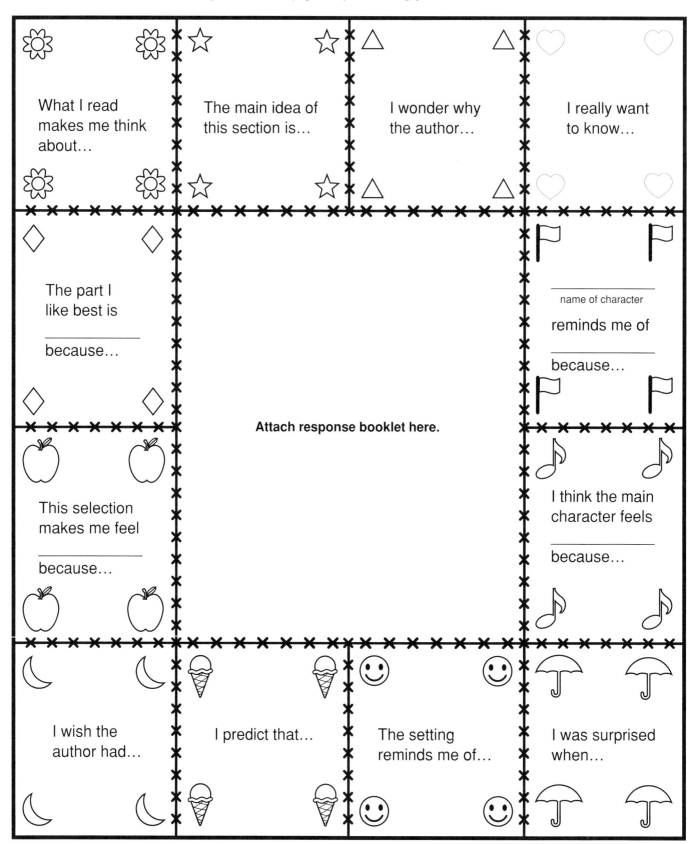

What I read makes me think about…

The main idea of this section is…

I wonder why the author…

I really want to know…

The part I like best is _____ because…

Attach response booklet here.

_____
name of character
reminds me of _____ because…

This selection makes me feel _____ because…

I think the main character feels _____ because…

I wish the author had…

I predict that…

The setting reminds me of…

I was surprised when…

The Best of The Mailbox® • Grades 4–6 • ©The Mailbox® Books • TEC61169

134   **Note to the teacher:** Use with "Response Quilt" on page 132.

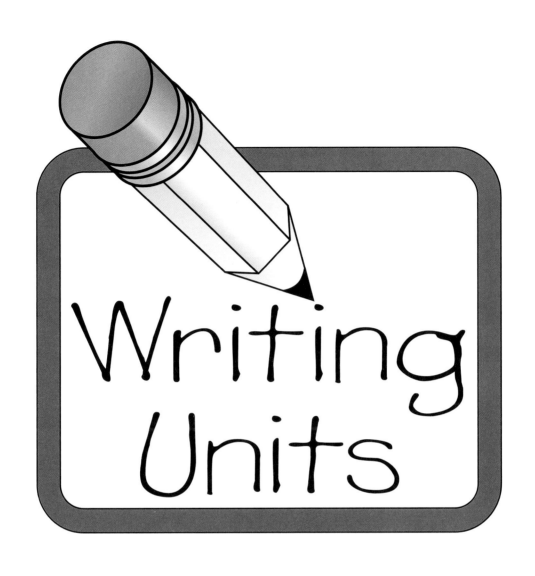

Writing Units

"Write" From the Start

Activities to Teach Prewriting Strategies

Sometimes the hardest part of writing isn't writing; it's the thinking and planning that come before you ever pick up a pen or touch a keyboard. Use the following activities to teach your students prewriting strategies that will help them get off to the "write" start!

with ideas by Marcia Barton, Cocoa Beach, FL

"What do I write about?"

Focusing on the Fundamentals

Skills: Choosing a specific subject, idea development

Young writers often succumb to the "I-don't-know-what-to-write-about" blues. Help your kids overcome this obstacle by teaching them a surefire strategy for identifying a specific subject to write about. In advance, make a transparency of page 138. Point out the gameboard illustrated on the page and read the steps with students. Then have one child roll two dice. Beginning at Start, count the number of gameboard spaces rolled. Then write the matching fundamental area of life in the blank in Step 1. Work with the class to complete the rest of the page as directed. Explain that thinking about a fundamental area of life can help a writer identify a number of interesting and specific writing topics. End the activity by having each student complete a copy of page 138 on his own. If desired, post a list of the fundamentals of life in your classroom so students can refer to it when the "I-don't-know-what-to-write-about" blues hit.

Subjects

my best friend
our school
television
computers
pets
freedom
helping others

MY BEST FRIEND

the day I met my best friend
my best friend's bedroom
my best friend's sense of humor
my best friend's pesky little brother
what I like most about my best friend
my first fight with my best friend
my best friend's messy closet
qualities of a best friend

This Topic's Too Big!

Skills: Choosing a specific subject, idea development

When it comes to choosing a subject to write about, students often mistakenly think bigger is better. Use the following activity to practice cutting big subjects down to size. Write each subject shown at the top of a separate chart. Then tape the charts around the room. Discuss the subjects with students, leading them to conclude that each one is too big to cover in one writing assignment. Choose one chart and ask students to suggest more specific subjects to list on it (see the example).

Next, divide the class into groups. Give each group a different-colored marker and send it to a different poster. Set a timer for three minutes. Then challenge each group to list as many specific writing subjects as possible on its chart. When time is up, signal each group to move to another chart. Allow two minutes for reading the chart (so that ideas won't be duplicated). Then set the timer for three minutes again and repeat the activity. Continue until each group has contributed to every chart. Discuss the subjects students listed on each chart to determine whether they are specific enough. Then, if desired, have each child choose one subject to write about. *adapted from an idea by Mary Skelly, Salem Central School, Salem, NY*

"On-Line" Help

Skills: Gathering details about the subject, idea development

Each student has selected a specific subject to write about. Now it's time to gather details, which is an especially important step if students are writing research reports or other informational pieces. To encourage students to help each other with this step, stretch two clotheslines across a bulletin board titled "'On-Line' Help." Make sure the lines are securely attached and within students' reach. Clip a class supply of small clothespins on the lines. Then have each student attach to a clothesline a sheet of paper labeled with his writing subject and name.

During free time, a classmate reads a student's subject. Then she lists on a separate piece of paper questions or other details about the subject (including suggestions about sources of information the writer might find helpful). Finally, the student staples her paper behind the classmate's paper and returns it to the clothesline. After at least two peers have added their ideas, the first student removes his paper from the clothesline. Then he uses the suggestions to help him plan his writing.

My writing subject is <u>pollution in our state</u>.

Kevin

There is plenty of pollution in the Kentucky River. My uncle lives by the river and could give you an interview.

Bethany

Analyze This!

Skills: Gathering details about the subject, idea development

Asking analytical questions is a great way to gather details for a writing assignment. To give your kids a chance to try this questioning strategy, divide the class into pairs and give each child the materials listed. Post the questions shown. Then guide students through the steps below. At the end of the activity, have students store the question cards in their writing folders to use with the next writing assignment.

Materials for each student: 6 index cards, tape, pencil, paper, highlighter

Steps:
1. Write each question on a separate index card.
2. Tape the cards as shown. Then fold them accordion-style in a stack.
3. Ask your partner each question on your cards. Listen carefully to the answers and take notes on your paper.
4. Switch roles and repeat Step 3.
5. Give your partner the notes you took on his subject.
6. Read the notes your partner took on your subject. Highlight the details you'd like to include in your writing assignment.

1. When you think about your subject, what do you see? Hear? Smell? Feel? Taste?

2. What is your subject similar to? Different from?

3. What does your subject make you think of?

Questions
1. When you think about your subject, what do you see? Hear? Smell? Feel? Taste?
2. What is your subject similar to? Different from?
3. What does your subject make you think of?
4. Is your subject useful? Why or why not?
5. What parts make up your subject?
6. Why is your subject important enough to write about?

Start

education   love   family   health

Name _____

Get Rolling!

"I don't know what to write about!" Ever feel that way? Most writers do at one time or another. When you need to find a specific subject to write about, get rolling by using the strategy below!

1. Each gameboard space lists a fundamental area of life. Choose one area and write it in the blank. _____

2. Think about the area you have listed. Then list three specific subjects you could write about that are related to the area. For example:

   Fundamental area: clothing
   Subject: the day in first grade when I had to wear a bunny costume on the bus
   Subject: the best brand of sneakers on the market today
   Subject: my aunt's collection of crazy hats

   a. _____

   b. _____

   c. _____

3. Choose a different area from the gameboard and write it in the blank. _____ Then list three specific subjects you could write about that are related to the area.

   a. _____

   b. _____

   c. _____

4. Draw a star beside the subject you'd most like to write about.

Bonus Box: Choose an area from the gameboard. On the back of this page, list four different writing subjects that are related to that category. For example, if you select art and music, you might list "my weekend at art camp" or "my favorite radio station."

home   plants   travel   art and music   animals   friends

laws   hobbies   work   food   clothing   money

environment   technology   entertainment   communication

The Best of The Mailbox® • *Grades 4–6* • ©The Mailbox® Books • TEC61169

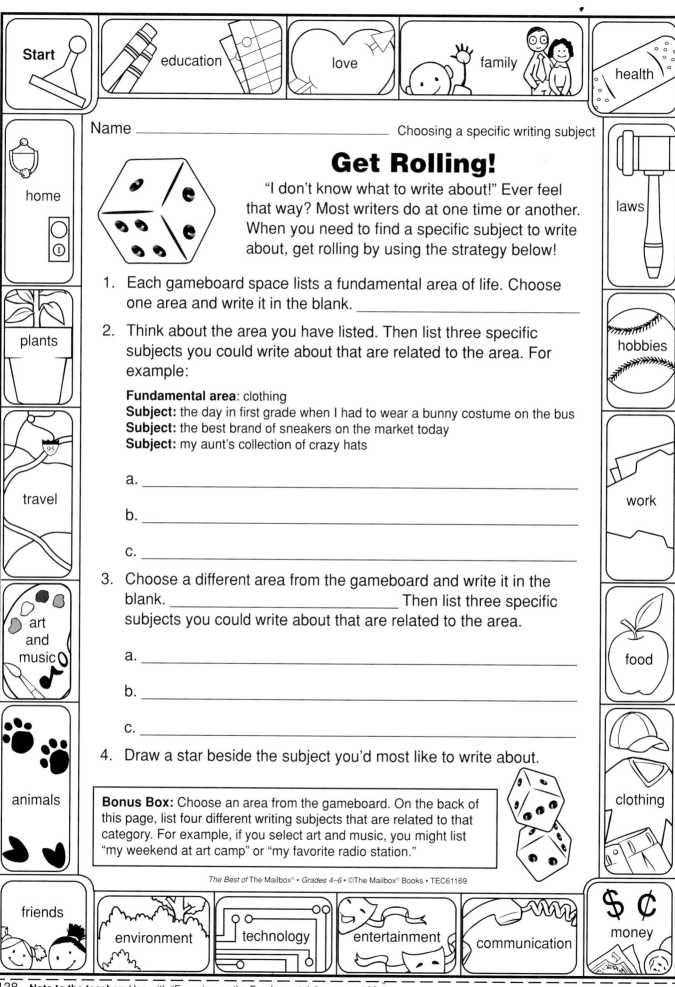

Painting With a Palette of Figurative Language

Just as painters choose colors to create pictures for the eye, writers must choose words to create pictures for the mind. Use this palette of figurative language activities to help your students become artists of the written word.

by Christa New, Staff Editor

"Hues" Your Senses

Skills: Recognizing imagery, writing a poem

Focus students' attention on recognizing imagery with this colorful poetry-writing activity. Begin by asking students to name their favorite colors. Ask them to explain why they like those colors and what they think of when they see them. Then share with the class several poems from *Hailstones and Halibut Bones* by Mary O'Neill. Discuss with students how the author uses *imagery* to write about colors. Explain that imagery is the way a writer uses words to help the reader imagine how something looks, smells, feels, tastes, or sounds. Have students point out ways that the author used imagery in the poems you shared.

Next, have each student complete a chart about a color of her choice and how it affects her senses and emotions (see the example). Afterward, direct the student to use the chart to help her write a poem similar to those penned by Mary O'Neill. Finally, have each student write and illustrate her poem on a copy of the palette pattern on page 142. Now that's "hues-ing" your senses!

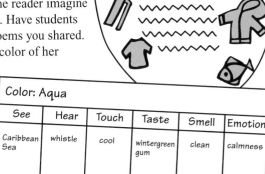

What Is Aqua?

Color: Aqua

See	Hear	Touch	Taste	Smell	Emotion
Caribbean Sea	whistle	cool	wintergreen gum	clean	calmness

I'm starving! I think I'll have pizza for lunch.

Gurgle!

Grrrrr!

The Eye, the Ear, and the Art

Skills: Using onomatopoeia, writing a poem

Introduce students to onomatopoeia and some famous works of art with a writing activity that sounds picture-perfect! First, ask your art teacher to provide you with several prints of well-known masterpieces or show examples from any of the following books by Lucy Micklethwait: *A Child's Book of Art: Discover Great Paintings*, *A Child's Book of Art*, or *I Spy: An Alphabet in Art* (I Spy series). Discuss the paintings with your students by pointing out the subjects, settings, and colors.

Next, choose one painting and have students imagine that they are the artist. Ask, "What sounds did you hear as you were painting this picture?" List students' responses on chart paper. Explain that *onomatopoeia* is using words whose sounds indicate their meanings, such as *buzz, purr, thump,* and *snap.* Then have each student choose a masterpiece and list sounds that she might have heard if she had been the artist who created that painting. Afterward, instruct her to write a poem about the painting that includes examples of onomatopoeia. Display the completed poems around the featured works of art after students share them with the class.

139

Puzzling Portraits
Skill: Writing with similes and metaphors

Create perfectly puzzling portraits with this simile and metaphor activity! Review with students that a *simile* compares two unlike things using the words *like* or *as,* while a *metaphor* compares two unlike things without using either of those words. Next, direct each student to write—but not sign—a brief paragraph that uses only similes and metaphors to describe her physical appearance (see the example at the right). Afterward, collect and randomly redistribute the papers, making sure that no student receives her own. Also give each child a sheet of white paper and crayons or colored pencils. Have the student read the description she's been given and draw a silly portrait based on it (see the example). Finally, display the portraits on a bulletin board titled "Perfectly Puzzling Portraits" and see whether each subject can recognize herself!

My eyes are dark tunnels burrowing into the back of my head. My hair is as curly as a pig's tail. My nose is covered with a blanket of leopard spots. My cheeks are rosy like the sunset. My mouth is like a small strawberry.

The fisherman caught a whale of a fish!

I am so hungry, I could eat a horse!

My grandmother cooked enough food to feed an entire army!

Susie talks a mile a minute.

I ate so much that I think I'm going to burst!

Our telephone rings off the hook.

Amy's scared to death of spiders.

My little cousin is just knee-high to a grasshopper.

Mary is pencil thin.

My brother drives his car so fast that the tires catch on fire!

Ellen's nose is always in a book.

The temperature is going to be boiling hot tomorrow.

I'm so tired, I could fall asleep standing up.

I've told you a million times to stop doing that!

Greg died laughing.

Really! It Was This Big!
Skills: Using hyperbole, writing a tall tale

Give your students a chance to really stretch the truth with this creative-writing activity! Ahead of time, write each hyperbole shown at the left on a different index card and place the cards in an envelope. Next, share several tall tales with your students. Ask students to identify examples of exaggeration in the stories. Explain that each exaggeration is a figure of speech called a *hyperbole*. Then pair students. Have each pair draw a card from the envelope and write a story in which that hyperbole is presented as a true event. After each story has been written, give each twosome a supply of 9" x 12" white paper and crayons. Direct the pair to rewrite and illustrate its story in picture-book format. Then watch the authors' heads swell with pride as they share their hyperbolic tales with the class!

Say That Three Times Fast!
Skill: Using alliteration

Accentuate alliteration with this amusing activity! First, write several tongue twisters on the board, such as "Sally sells seashells by the seashore," "Peter Piper picked a peck of pickled peppers," and "Five fat frogs fly past fast." Challenge students to quickly say each tongue twister three times. Then ask what makes a tongue twister so hard to say. *(It strings words together that have the same initial sound.)* Explain that *alliteration* is the repetition of beginning consonant sounds in words. Point out the alliteration in each tongue twister on the board. Then instruct each student to write a tongue twister about himself. Have him use as many words as possible that begin with the first letter of his first name. Then have the student write and illustrate his tongue twister on a 12" x 18" sheet of white paper. Display the finished pieces of alliterative art on a bulletin board titled "Awesome Alliteration." *Julia Alarie, Essex Middle School, Essex, VT*

Beautiful Becky Beauregard bounced blue beach balls behind bashful Bart's broken-down brown barn.

Personification Persuasion

Skills: Using personification, creating a commercial

Use this creative group activity to set the stage for understanding personification. First, explain to students that *personification* is a figure of speech in which an object, idea, or animal is given characteristics of a person. For example, in the commercial for Mrs. Butterworth's pancake syrup, the syrup bottle speaks and moves like a human. Have students brainstorm examples of personification in other television commercials—such as the talking M&M's candies and Poppin' Fresh, the Pillsbury Doughboy—as you write them on the board.

Next, divide students into small groups. Instruct each group to select a familiar product and create a commercial for it using personification. Direct the group to write a script for the commercial that includes props and, if desired, music. Then have each group rehearse its commercial and perform it for the class.

Idiom Fast Draw

Skill: Recognizing idioms

This game can make recognizing idioms as easy as pie! First, make a copy of the idiom cards below for each pair of teams. Place each set of cards in a separate bag. Next, divide students into teams of four players; then pair teams to play. Give each pair of teams a bag of idiom cards, markers, and drawing paper. To play:

1. Player 1 from Team 1 draws a card from the bag and reads it silently.
2. Player 1 illustrates the idiom on the paper in one minute or less. Team 1 tries to guess the correct idiom as it's being drawn. If Team 1 guesses correctly, it receives one point. If it can also correctly explain the idiom's meaning, it receives a bonus point. The team asks the teacher to settle any disagreements over an idiom's meaning.
3. If Team 1 doesn't guess correctly before a minute is up, Team 2 guesses and receives a point if correct. Team 2 may also try for the bonus point.
4. Team 2 takes a turn in the same manner.
5. Play continues until all the cards have been used. The team with more points is the winner.

Idiom Cards

Use with "Idiom Fast Draw" on this page.

elbow grease TEC61169	thank your lucky stars TEC61169	hold your tongue TEC61169	have a ball TEC61169
easy as pie TEC61169	hit the books TEC61169	frog in my throat TEC61169	put my foot in my mouth TEC61169
stick to your guns TEC61169	sticky fingers TEC61169	in the doghouse TEC61169	eagle eye TEC61169
wild goose chase TEC61169	bite my head off TEC61169	lend a hand TEC61169	have ants in your pants TEC61169
green thumb TEC61169	out to lunch TEC61169	sweet tooth TEC61169	raining cats and dogs TEC61169

Palette Pattern

Use with "'Hues' Your Senses" on page 139.

That's One Amazing Dog!

Here's your chance to stretch the truth and get away with it! Describe an amazing dog by writing a hyperbole to complete each sentence below. Remember that the more you exaggerate, the better the hyperbole will be!

1. My dog is so beautiful _____

2. My dog is so smart _____

3. My dog is so strong _____

4. My dog is so friendly _____

5. My dog runs so fast _____

6. My dog is so sweet _____

7. My dog is so talented _____

8. My dog is so well trained _____

9. My dog is so cool _____

10. My dog is so funny _____

11. My dog is so popular _____

12. My dog loves me so much _____

Bonus Box: Write three exaggerated compliments that you'd love to hear your best friend say about you. Write them on the back of this page.

The Best of The Mailbox® • *Grades 4–6* • ©The Mailbox® Books • TEC61169

Fishing for Figurative Language

As you read the following story, be on the lookout for different types of figurative language. Then underline each example according to the code.

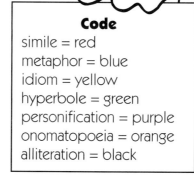

Code
simile = red
metaphor = blue
idiom = yellow
hyperbole = green
personification = purple
onomatopoeia = orange
alliteration = black

As the sun peeked over the horizon, Andy Allen and Amy Atwater were already headed for the lake. Today was the Lucky Lure fishing tournament, and they wanted to be at their favorite spot early. As their truck rounded the last bend in the road, they spotted the lake. The aqua-blue water was a shiny mirror. What a perfect day for fishing!

As quick as a wink, Andy launched the boat in the water while Amy sorted the rods and reels. Andy gunned the engine and the boat shot off like a rocket. But as they came around the corner, Andy and Amy spied another boat at their favorite fishing spot! Their hearts dropped like rocks, and they knew they were in a pickle.

"Where will we fish?" Andy asked Amy.

"Sit tight," Amy replied. "I think I may have another trick up my sleeve."

Amy directed Andy to a small cove on the other side of the lake. Lily pads floated like saucers on the water and birds chirped cheerfully all around them. Andy picked up his rod and cast it toward the moss-covered bank. Kerplunk! The lure splashed into the water. Before Andy had time to blink, his line began to zing. He had a fish!

"Amy!" hollered Andy excitedly. "Lend me a hand and grab the net!" Andy reeled and reeled but the fish fought him tooth and nail. Andy began sweating bullets. He knew the tournament victory would depend on this catch.

Suddenly, he and Amy received a stroke of luck! The fish began to tire of struggling and drifted toward the surface. Amy leaned over the boat and grabbed the fish with the net.

"Andy, you lucky dog," exclaimed Amy. "You caught a whale of a fish! You're sure to win the tournament now."

"But you helped me catch him," replied Andy. "We'll share the prize."

Amy and Andy zoomed back to the dock to weigh their fish and claim the prize: a Lucky Lure fishing hat and T-shirt.

"Wow! What a wonderful day," said Andy as they drove home. "But I'm exhausted."

"Me too," Amy said with a yawn. "But let's come back tomorrow and see if there are any more whales in that cove!"

The Best of The Mailbox® • *Grades 4–6* • ©The Mailbox® Books • TEC61169 • Key p. 189

Note to the teacher: Each student will need red, blue, yellow, green, purple, orange, and black crayons (or markers or colored pencils) to complete this page.

Ten "Pen-tastic" Ways to Improve Journal Writing

Give your journal-writing program a boost with ten terrific tips
that can inspire in your students a lifelong love of writing!

by Daniel Kriesberg, Bayville, NY

1. Take advantage of tiny bits of time. Even if a busy class schedule leaves you with only ten minutes once a week or five minutes here and there for impromptu writing, giving students a small amount of time to write is better than none at all. Train your students to whip out their journals and begin writing whenever you say, "Journal time!"

2. Use a class journal to model journal writing. Teach students how to write in a journal by using chart paper. Ask students to call out entries one at a time for you to record. Or invite each child to come up and write his entry on the chart paper. As this is being done, explain your expectations or model one of the other tips on these pages.

3. Display and discuss the journals of other writers. Inspire students to write in their journals by showing them your own journal or one published by a famous author or scientist. Or ask friends or family members if you can share excerpts from their journals. Then discuss the different topics people write about or the writing styles they use.

4. Encourage visits to online journal sites. Suggest that students visit Web sites you have preapproved to see how some people have used journals, diaries, and letters to record memories about hiking the Appalachian Trail or traveling the Oregon Trail.

5. Share inspirational picture books. Motivate students by sharing picture books that inspire journal writing, such as *I'm in Charge of Celebrations* by Byrd Baylor and *An Island Scrapbook: Dawn to Dusk on a Barrier Island* by Virginia Wright-Frierson.

6. Suggest that students occasionally make lists. Post a list of topics such as the following: animals I have seen, places I have been, goals I'd like to reach, jokes I like, sports I play, books I have read. Then have each writer complete an entry using single words or short phrases instead of complete sentences or paragraphs.

7. Challenge students to go beyond a simple accounting of a day's events. Gently push students to dig deeper and use richer descriptions when they write in their journals. Begin by having each writer describe an everyday object such as a spoon, using as much detail as possible. The next day, ask the writer to add to her description. Then have her go back a third time and write even more. Help students understand that the closer they look, the more they will find to write about!

8. Take students outside to sharpen their senses. Have them sit under a tree and watch younger children at recess or notice insects crawling on the ground. Students could even listen to all the sounds around them or look for shapes in the clouds. Return to the same spot often so students can observe the changes that occur.

9. Permit students to add sketches and illustrations to their journals. Accept the fact that words are not the only way to record memories, thoughts, or observations. Allowing students to include drawings—even colorful ones—in their journals helps them become better observers.

10. Allow items to be glued to the pages. If a child understands that he can add personal items—such as small mementos, maps, photographs, or ticket stubs—to a journal, he is more likely to turn it into a treasured keepsake.

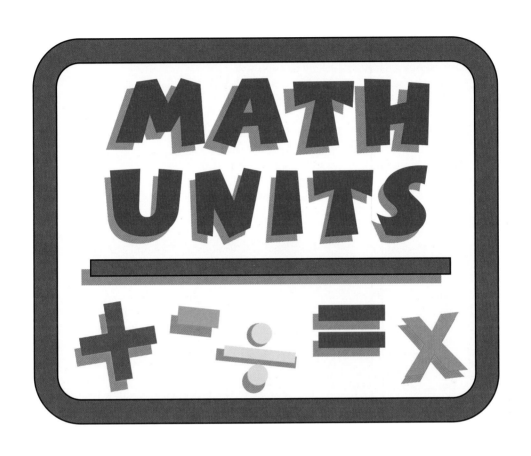

"Fin-tastic" Ways to Practice Multiplication Facts

Dive into a refreshing pool of activities that are perfect for practicing multiplication facts and can be adapted for other facts as well!

What Time Is It?

Practicing multiplication facts is just a tick away with this **timely activity!** Announce that several times during the school day you will ask, "What time is it?" Explain that when this happens, you will call on someone to find the product of the two numbers the hands on the classroom clock are pointing to (or are closest to). For example, at 9:15 A.M., the clock's hands point to 9 and 3, so a student would say, "Nine times three equals 27." At first, ask the question two or three times each hour. Then taper off to several times a week. With digital clocks, have students multiply the hour by the minute's tens-place digit and then by its ones-place digit. So what time is it? *Rebecca McCright, Henderson Elementary, Midland, TX*

> Nine times three equals 27.

Rollin' With the Facts

What do multiplication flash cards, a die, index cards, plus a small group of students add up to? Piles of fun **facts practice!** Begin by drawing a different die face on each of six index cards. Arrange the flash cards in six piles and place an index card atop each pile. Next, have a child roll the die and take a flash card from the rolled number's pile. Direct the child to read the card aloud and say its product. If correct, allow the player to keep the card. If incorrect, instruct him to place the card at the bottom of that number's pile. Then have the next player roll the die and take his turn. If there are no more cards in the rolled number's pile, a player loses his turn. When all cards have been claimed, declare the player with the most cards the winner! *Sharyn Jontz, Winter Park, FL*

Multiplication War

Declare all-out war on multiplication facts with this **competitive card game!** Pair students. Have each player stack ten flash cards, equation side up, in front of her. Instruct Player A to place her top card in the middle of the table, read its fact, and say its product. Player B turns the card over to check the answer. Player B takes her turn in a similar manner. The player whose card has the greater product gets to keep both cards. If the cards' products are equal, have the players declare war by stacking four cards each in the center of the table and using only the products of the fourth cards to break the tie. Direct both players to return those cards to the bottom of their piles. Then continue play in the manner described until all of the cards have been captured. Declare the player with more cards the winner! *Stacy Shaener, Riverside Elementary, Greenwich, CT*

> I get both cards because my product is greater!

6 x 9

6 x 7

4 x 6

3 x 9

$6 \times 5 = 30$

Magic number: 12

$12 \times 6 = 72$
$12 \times 3 = 36$
$12 \times 10 = 120$
$12 \times 7 = 84$

Magic-Number Multiplication

Make practicing multiplication facts magical with this "cap-tivating" **partner game!** Ask parents to send in clean caps from plastic jugs and bottles. Label each cap's top with a number from 0 to 12. Give each child a handful of caps to place number-side down on his desk. Direct him to pick up any cap and use it as the magic number by which he multiplies each of the other caps' numbers (see the example). After practicing in this way several times, pair students. Make sure that partners have the same number of caps. At your signal, have each partner repeat the steps he practiced. Award a point to the first player in each pair who multiplies the facts correctly. Play several rounds. Then declare the player with more points in each pair the winner! *Amber Jenkins, Smith Elementary, Richmond, TX*

$7 \times 1 = 7$

Clapping for Multiples

Give your students practice with multiplication tables one clap at a time! For this **whole-group game,** direct each student to stand behind his chair. Name a number from 1 to 12. Then have children count off beginning with 1. When a student reaches a number that is a multiple of the original number named, direct him to clap one time instead of naming the multiple. For example, if you named the number 6, the children who reach 6, 12, 24, and so on should each clap one time. Continue having each student call out a number or clap until 12 times the number has been reached. If a child incorrectly names a number or claps, have her sit down. Play as many rounds as desired, changing the original number named each time. *Irene Taylor, Fort Ann, NY*

1 2 3 4 5 CLAP

"Tower-ful" Facts

Strengthen students' skills with multiplication facts by using a tower of **blocks** from a Jenga game! Label each block's sides and ends with the product of a different multiplication fact. Have students build one or more towers (one with 18 stories, two with nine stories, or three with six stories). To play, have one player call out a fact whose product is not written on the tower's top layer. Have the player on his left locate the block with the matching answer, remove it, and stack it carefully on the top of the tower to start a new layer. Continue having students take turns in this manner until the tower falls. Declare the last player to take a turn without making the tower fall the winner! *Kim Brown, Mounds, OK*

149

Name _____

Swimmin' to School

Freddy doesn't know the way to his new school. Show him the path by using a blue crayon to color the bubble of each correct multiplication fact. Then answer the riddle by writing the letter found inside each colored bubble in order on the lines below.

6 x 9 = 54 **R**	8 x 6 = 48 **E**	3 x 9 = 27 **A**	4 x 8 = 32 **L**

8 x 9 = 78 **S**	7 x 7 = 42 **U**	4 x 7 = 21 **P**	8 x 8 = 65 **E**	6 x 7 = 48 **R**	5 x 8 = 40 **L**

9 x 9 = 81 **A**	12 x 12 = 144 **T**	10 x 10 = 100 **N**	4 x 9 = 36 **I**	6 x 6 = 36 **F**	4 x 6 = 24 **Y**

7 x 5 = 35 **S**	3 x 8 = 26 **B**	4 x 4 = 18 **O**	0 x 8 = 8 **R**	3 x 7 = 24 **E**

Under-the-Sea School

3 x 3 = 6 **D**	4 x 5 = 20 **T**	8 x 7 = 56 **I**	9 x 7 = 63 **C**

What did Freddy say about his first day at the school?

It was ___ ___ ___ ___ ___   " ___ ___ ___ - ___ ___ ___ ___ ___ ___ ___ "!

Bonus Box: Replace each incorrect answer in the uncolored bubbles above with the correct answer.

The Best of The Mailbox® • *Grades 4–6* • ©The Mailbox® Books • TEC61169 • Key p. 189

Note to the teacher: Each student will need a blue crayon to complete this page.

Star-Spangled Coordinate Graphing

Make students' understanding of coordinate graphing shine even brighter with this sparkling collection of out-of-this-world activities!

by Melissa H. Bryan, Valley Forge Middle School, Wayne, PA

(4,4)

(2,10)

(6,8)

(10,0)

Coordinated Footsteps

Identifying ordered pairs of whole numbers on a grid

Discover how a few small steps on a classroom floor grid can lead to a giant leap in students' understanding of coordinate graphing! Enlarge and make ten copies of the footprint pattern shown. After cutting out the footprints and labeling them with the letters *A–J*, affix masking tape to your classroom floor to form a 10 x 10 grid. Use a marker to number the axes from 0 to 10. Place the cutouts on the grid at different intersections. Call on one student to provide the ordered pair that identifies a particular footprint's location. Call on another student to take that number of steps on the grid across and up from zero to check the answer. Repeat until every letter's location has been correctly identified. Continue in this manner, rearranging the cutouts on the grid as needed, until every child has had a turn. Conclude by having each student describe on paper how to determine a point's coordinates on a grid.

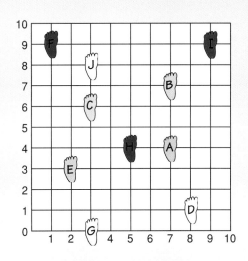

Crater Coordinates

Locating ordered pairs of whole numbers on a grid

This coordinate-graphing activity will have students smiling at the man in the moon! Have students bring in clean, empty egg cartons until there are three cartons for each child. Next, direct each student to cut off the lids and arrange the carton bottoms to form a 6 x 6 grid as shown. Explain that the grid represents the moon's craters. Then give each student a handful of two-color counters. Explain that the counters represent moon rocks that can rest in the moon's craters. Call out the following ordered pairs one at a time, and have each student place a counter red-side up in the matching crater of her grid: (1, 3), (2, 2), (2, 6), (3, 1), (3, 4), (4, 1), (4, 4), (5, 2), (5, 6), (6, 3). If students place counters in the correct craters, they'll see a smiling face (the man in the moon). Follow up by having each child create and record the matching ordered pairs for a different design that a partner can try to re-create!

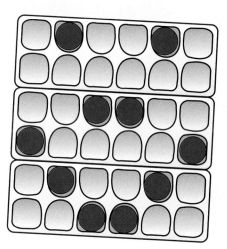

151

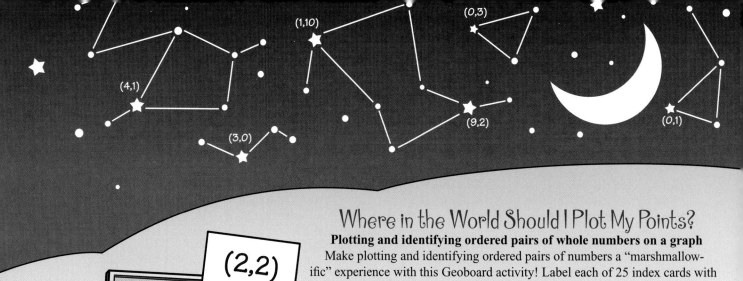

(4,1)

(3,0)

(1,10)

(0,3)

(9,2)

(0,1)

Where in the World Should I Plot My Points?

Plotting and identifying ordered pairs of whole numbers on a graph

Make plotting and identifying ordered pairs of numbers a "marshmallow-ific" experience with this Geoboard activity! Label each of 25 index cards with a different ordered pair from (0, 0) to (4, 4). Also wrap the first row and column of each student's Geoboard with rubber bands to create axes. Then give each child a Geoboard and eight mini marshmallows (four white, four colored). Have her place the white marshmallows on any four neighboring pegs. Next, draw a card and announce its ordered pair. If a child has a marshmallow on that peg, have her replace it with a colored marshmallow. Continue calling out ordered pairs in this manner until one child has replaced all four white marshmallows with colored ones and calls out, "Four points plotted!" Instruct her to state the coordinates of her pairs. If they match, allow her to be the next caller!

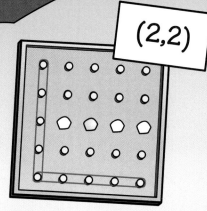

(2,2)

Decoding Messages From Space

Plotting ordered pairs of whole numbers on a grid

Help students get the point about plotting ordered pairs of numbers with a banner-making activity! Divide students into groups of four or five. Give each group member a 10 x 10 grid. Instruct him to number the grid's axes from 0 to 10. Next, have the group choose a word with the same number of letters as people in its group. Have each group member illustrate a different letter of the word by plotting successive points on his grid and listing the matching ordered pairs below the grid as shown. After group members check each other's work, have them tape their grids together to form a banner that spells their word. Then invite the groups to read each other's words!

(1, 1), (1, 2), (1, 3), (1, 4), (1, 5), (1, 6),
(1, 7), (1, 8), (1, 9), (1, 10), (2, 9), (3, 8),
(4, 7), (5, 6), (6, 7), (7, 8), (8, 9), (9, 10),
(9, 9), (9, 8), (9, 7), (9, 6), (9, 5), (9, 4),
(9, 3), (9, 2), (9, 1)

(2, 1), (2, 2), (2, 3), (2, 4), (2, 5), (2, 6),
(3, 4), (3, 7), (4, 4), (4, 8), (5, 4), (5, 9),
(6, 4), (6, 8), (7, 4), (7, 7), (8, 6), (8, 5),
(8, 4), (8, 3), (8, 2), (8, 1)

(2, 9), (3, 9), (4, 9), (5, 1), (5, 2), (5, 3),
(5, 4), (5, 5), (5, 6), (5, 7), (5, 8), (5, 9),
(6, 9), (7, 9), (8, 9)

(2, 1), (2, 2), (2, 3), (2, 4), (2, 5), (2, 6),
(2, 7), (2, 8), (2, 9), (3, 5), (4, 5), (5, 5),
(6, 5), (7, 5), (8, 5), (9, 9), (9, 8), (9, 7),
(9, 6), (9, 5), (9, 4), (9, 3), (9, 2), (9, 1)

Seeing Stars

Triangulum

Dr. Luke Stargazer fell on his way to work this morning. Now he's having trouble plotting and identifying the constellations he needs for a lecture. Help him out!

Directions: For problems 1–3, plot a point for each ordered pair. Connect the points on each grid, in order, to draw three different constellations. For problems 4–6, identify each constellation by writing the letter for each ordered pair in its matching blank.

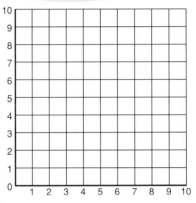

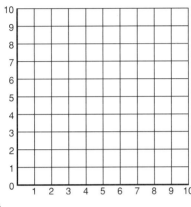

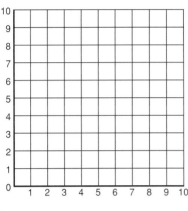

1 (8, 10), (8, 9), (9, 7), (9, 5), (8, 4), (7, 4), (5, 4), (4, 6), (3, 6), (2, 6), (1, 5), (2, 4), (4, 1), (5, 1), (5, 0), (4, 0), (4, 1)

2 (0, 9), (1, 9), (3, 8), (4, 7), (4, 5), (8, 5), (9, 7), (4, 7)

3 (6, 1), (6, 2), (4, 4), (4, 6), (3, 6), (3, 7), (2, 7), (2, 8)

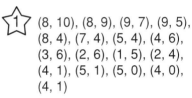

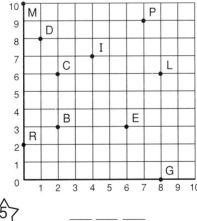

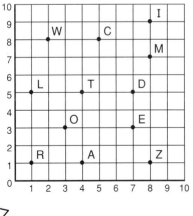

4 $\overline{\quad}$ $\overline{\quad}$ $\overline{\quad}$ $\overline{\quad}$ $\overline{\quad}$ $\overline{\quad}$
(2, 9) (3, 3) (1, 6) (6, 2) (5, 8) (1, 0)

5 $\overline{\quad}$ $\overline{\quad}$ $\overline{\quad}$
(2, 3) (4, 7) (8, 0)

6 $\overline{\quad}$ $\overline{\quad}$ $\overline{\quad}$ $\overline{\quad}$ $\overline{\quad}$ $\overline{\quad}$ $\overline{\quad}$
(1, 5) (4, 1) (5, 8) (7, 3) (1, 1) (4, 5) (4, 1)

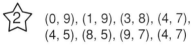

$\overline{\quad}$ $\overline{\quad}$ $\overline{\quad}$ $\overline{\quad}$ $\overline{\quad}$ $\overline{\quad}$
(1, 8) (4, 7) (7, 9) (7, 9) (6, 3) (0, 2)

Bonus Box: To find out another name for the constellation in problem 6, write the letters for the following ordered pairs: $\overline{\quad}$ $\overline{\quad}$ $\overline{\quad}$ $\overline{\quad}$ $\overline{\quad}$ $\overline{\quad}$.
　　　　　　(1, 5)　(8, 9)　(8, 1)　(4, 1)　(1, 1)　(7, 5)

The Fractions Speedway

Keep students' basic fraction skills on course with these action-packed maneuvers!

by Melissa Bryan, Valley Forge Middle School, Wayne, PA

Rarin' to Reduce!

Identifying and writing fractions in simplest form

You'll cause a race to the starting line with this simplifying-fractions activity! On chart paper, list simplified fractions such as those shown. Next, give each child a large handful of small different-colored manipulatives, such as gram unit cubes, color tiles, or Unifix cubes. Announce any manipulative color. Have each student find what fraction of his manipulatives is that color and then mentally reduce that fraction to its simplest form. If his simplified fraction is listed in the chart, have him write its unsimplified form in the matching row. Discuss any fractions students could not list on the chart and why (fractions were already in simplest form or represented an uncommon fraction, such as $\frac{2}{11}$). Repeat the process four times to generate as many different equivalent fractions as possible. Then display the chart as a ready reference.

Fractions	Simplest Form
$\frac{2}{4}$, $\frac{3}{6}$, $\frac{4}{8}$, $\frac{5}{10}$, $\frac{6}{12}$	$\frac{1}{2}$
$\frac{2}{6}$, $\frac{3}{9}$, $\frac{4}{12}$	$\frac{1}{3}$
$\frac{4}{6}$, $\frac{6}{9}$	$\frac{2}{3}$
$\frac{2}{8}$, $\frac{3}{12}$	$\frac{1}{4}$
$\frac{6}{8}$, $\frac{9}{12}$	$\frac{3}{4}$
$\frac{2}{10}$	$\frac{1}{5}$

Fraction Bow Ties

Comparing fractions

Refuel students' understanding of comparing fractions with a shortcut method that will have them looking quite dapper! Demonstrate the bow tie method using the fractions and directions shown. Then give each child a loop of masking tape and a large, colorful bow tie cutout. Instruct the student to write on her cutout two fractions and then tape the bow tie to her clothing. Next, have her walk around and copy ten problems from her classmates' bow ties onto a sheet of paper. Afterward, instruct her to return to her seat and compare the fractions using the shortcut method. When she's done, have her compare the fractions on her own bow tie. After you check it, have her pin the cutout to a bulletin board titled as shown. Once all of the bow ties are in place, students can check their ten problems by looking at the board!

$$24 \quad \tfrac{3}{4} \bowtie \tfrac{7}{8} \quad 28$$
$$24 < 28$$
$$\text{so } \tfrac{3}{4} < \tfrac{7}{8}$$

The Bow Tie Method

1. Multiply the first fraction's denominator by the second fraction's numerator. Record the product on the right.
2. Multiply the second fraction's denominator by the first fraction's numerator. Record the product on the left.
3. Compare the two products. Write "<," ">," or "=" between the fractions.

Dapper Comparisons

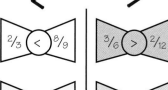

<	>	=
$\frac{2}{3} < \frac{8}{9}$	$\frac{3}{6} > \frac{2}{12}$	$\frac{3}{4} = \frac{9}{12}$
$\frac{2}{4} < \frac{5}{8}$	$\frac{5}{11} > \frac{3}{8}$	$\frac{1}{5} = \frac{2}{10}$

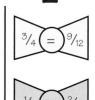
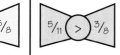

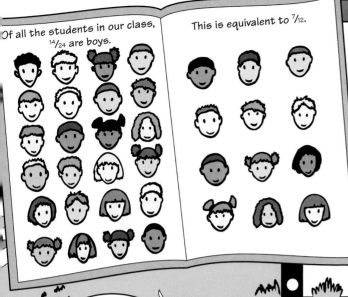

Of all the students in our class, ¹⁴/₂₄ are boys.

This is equivalent to ⁷/₁₂.

Finding Fellow Fractions

Finding equivalent fractions

Turn a practice lap with equivalent fractions into a class picture book! First, help students brainstorm real-life examples of using equivalent fractions and list them on the board. Generate enough ideas to have one example for every two students. Next, pair students and assign each twosome a different idea, such as the fraction of boys in the class or face cards in a deck of cards. Give each partner colorful markers and a sheet of drawing paper. Also review how to find equivalent fractions. Then have the duo discuss how to illustrate its assigned idea, plus the idea's equivalent representation (see the example). When everyone is finished, invite the partners to share their work with the class. Then compile the sheets into a book to share with other classes at your school!

⁴/₇ is closest to ¹/₂

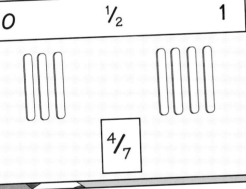

| 0 | ½ | 1 |

⁴/₇

Round to 0: ¹/₅, ¹/₆, ²/₇, ²/₉, ³/₁₀
Round to ½: ²/₅, ³/₅, ³/₇, ⁴/₇, ³/₈, ⁴/₉, ⁵/₉
Round to 1: ⁴/₅, ⁵/₆, ⁵/₇, ⁶/₇, ⁵/₈, ⁷/₉, ⁷/₁₀, ⁹/₁₀

Bound to Round

Rounding fractions to 0, ½, or 1

Accelerate students' rounding skills with this cooperative activity! Randomly list on the board the fractions shown (not the headings). Then pair students. Give each twosome ten craft sticks, one sentence strip, and ten index cards. Next, form groups of four by having each pair of students work with another duo. Direct each foursome to choose any ten fractions from the list. Have each pair in the foursome label its ten index cards with the chosen fractions. Also have each twosome label its sentence strip as shown. Then guide each duo through the steps below. When both pairs of students are finished, have them compare their piles of index cards. If their piles do not match, have the foursome work together, repeating the steps for each mismatched card until they agree on its placement.

Steps:
1. Select a fraction card and arrange below the sentence strip the same number of craft sticks as the fraction's denominator. If the denominator is an odd number, place one more than half of the sticks between ½ and 1. Place the remaining sticks between 0 and ½. If the denominator is an even number, place half of the sticks between 0 and ½. Place the remaining sticks between ½ and 1.
2. Look at the fraction's numerator. If it is less than the number of sticks between 0 and ½, stack the index card below 0 on the sentence strip. If it is the same or about the same as the number of sticks below 0 and ½ and ½ and 1, stack the card below ½. If it is more than the number of sticks between ½ and 1, stack the card below 1.
3. Repeat Steps 1 and 2 with the remaining nine cards.

Sweet Tooth Fractions

Jill E. Bean just loves working at her grandfather's candy shop. She keeps track of the candy in the jars. Her weekly candy count is due today. Help her complete this sweet task!

Write a fraction that shows each amount of candy.

1. white gumballs   _____
2. swirled mints   _____
3. marbled gumballs   _____
4. striped sticks   _____
5. striped mints   _____
6. round lollipops   _____

Gumballs

Mints

Stick Candy

Lollipops

Fruit Chewies   Sour Stars   Jelly Beans   Gummy Twirls

Draw and color the candies to show each amount.

7. $\frac{3}{7}$ of the sour stars are purple.

8. $\frac{2}{15}$ of the jelly beans are green.

9. $\frac{3}{10}$ of the fruit chewies are yellow.

10. $\frac{7}{9}$ of the gummy twirls are red.

Bonus Box: On the back of this page, write fractions that show the uncolored candies for problems 7–10.

The Best of The Mailbox® • *Grades 4–6* • ©The Mailbox® Books • TEC61169 • Key p. 189

Divvy It Up!

Divine Division Activities

Divisors	Dividends
6	228
7	329
8	128
9	207
10	670
11	506

COLOR-PACKED PRACTICE
Dividing by one and two digits

To give your next review session a colorful twist, label either a whiteboard, a sheet of chart paper, or a transparency with six divisors and six dividends in six different colors as shown. (When the colors match, the dividends should divide evenly. When the colors are mixed, the quotients should have remainders.) Have students solve problems with the numbers by calling out directions such as "Estimate the quotient of the blues" or "Find the quotient of black divided by red." Students will request this activity again and again!

Make dividing whole numbers a sweeter experience
with these dandy activities!

with ideas by Jennifer Otter, Oak Ridge, NC

Snack-Bag Problems

1. How many 15-piece packs can be made with all the cereal pieces? *(8 packs, 120 ÷ 15 = 8)*
2. How many 18-piece packs can be made with all the cereal pieces? *(6 packs with 12 cereal pieces left over, 120 ÷ 18 = 6 R12)*
3. If the cereal pieces are divided among 7 packs, how many pieces are in each pack? *(17 pieces per pack with 1 cereal piece left over, 120 ÷ 7 = 17 R1)*

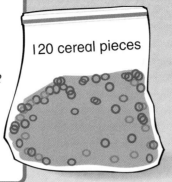

120 cereal pieces

Snack-Can Problems

1. How many 28 cm labels can be cut from a 252 cm strip of paper? *(9 labels, 252 ÷ 28 = 9)*
2. How many 22 cm labels can be cut from a 288 cm strip of paper? *(13 labels with 2 cm of paper left over, 288 ÷ 22 = 13 R2)*

MODEL MADNESS
Center

To help students represent division with models, stock a center with the following materials: a paper plate or paper towel to use as a workmat, a roll of adding machine tape, scissors, a ruler, and a resealable plastic bag labeled as shown and filled with 120 cereal rings. Introduce the center by announcing that a well-known packaging company needs students' help. Invite pairs of students to use the materials to solve the problems at the left and to record their work by writing a division sentence that represents each problem.

THREE IN A ROW
Partner game

In advance, make an adaptable gameboard by drawing a large 5 x 5 grid on a sheet of paper. Below the grid, copy from a math text 25 problems that you wish students to practice. Randomly write the answers in the grid's boxes. Then make a copy of the gameboard for each student pair. Give each twosome a gameboard, a calculator, and two different colored pencils. Direct each player to take a turn choosing a problem to solve and have his partner check the answer with the calculator. If the answer is correct, the solver uses his colored pencil to circle the correct answer and cross off the problem. If the answer is incorrect, the checker takes his turn. The first player to circle three quotients in a row in his color wins!

Box 'em Up!

Solve each problem. To match each can to its correct box below, look at each remainder. Label an unshaded circle in the corresponding box with that can's number. The first one has been done for you.

1.
$$7\overline{)548}\quad\text{78 R2}$$

2.
$$3\overline{)528}$$

3.
$$7\overline{)941}$$

4.
$$9\overline{)980}$$

5.
$$8\overline{)508}$$

6.
$$9\overline{)873}$$

10.
$$4\overline{)838}$$

9.
$$6\overline{)952}$$

8.
$$10\overline{)983}$$

7.
$$11\overline{)745}$$

11.
$$12\overline{)924}$$

12.
$$8\overline{)791}$$

13.
$$6\overline{)461}$$

14.
$$15\overline{)398}$$

No Remainder

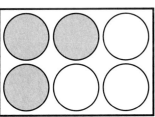

Remainder 1–3

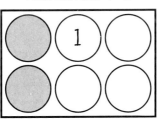

Remainder 4–6

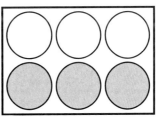

Remainder 7–9

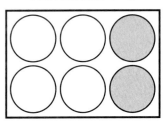

Monkeying Around With Measurement

Get into the swing of customary or metric measurement with these creative hands-on activities!

by Shawna Graham, The Colony, TX

Linear Designs

Measuring customary or metric units of length

Make practicing linear measurement more "a-peeling" with this fun-to-do activity! Give each student a sheet of drawing paper, a ruler, an index card, and an envelope. Instruct him to draw a small star somewhere on his paper. Then have him create a design that starts at the star and consists of connecting line segments that run north, south, east, or west (see the example). Direct the student to draw one segment at a time and label its length; then have him record on his index card the length of the segment and the direction in which it was drawn (as shown). When he is satisfied with his design, have the student fold it and place it and the directions in his envelope.

Next, give each child another sheet of drawing paper and have him trade envelopes with a classmate. Challenge each student to remove only the index card from the envelope and follow its directions to re-create his partner's design. To check, just have each student unfold the original drawing in the envelope and compare!

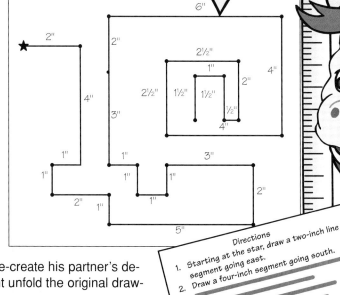

Directions
1. Starting at the star, draw a two-inch line segment going east.
2. Draw a four-inch segment going south.
3. _____
4. _____
5. _____
6. _____
7. _____
8. _____
9. _____

Do Size and Shape Matter?

Estimating and measuring customary or metric units of capacity

All you need for this eye-opening activity on capacity is a liquid measuring cup and a variety of empty containers. Have students bring in clean, empty containers of different sizes and shapes (with labels removed), such as a plastic soda bottle, peanut butter jar, or salad dressing bottle. When you have at least 15 containers, number each one with a marker and randomly display them in front of the room.

Next, divide the class into pairs. Challenge the partners to discuss each container's size and shape. Then have the pairs list the containers' numbers in order from least to greatest capacity. When everyone is finished, discuss students' rankings. Then, starting with the container predicted to have the smallest capacity, fill each container with water and have volunteers measure and record the results on the board. Ask other volunteers to adjust the containers' arrangement, if needed, to keep them in order by capacity. Once the arrangement is correct, have students discuss the outcome and which containers deceived them.

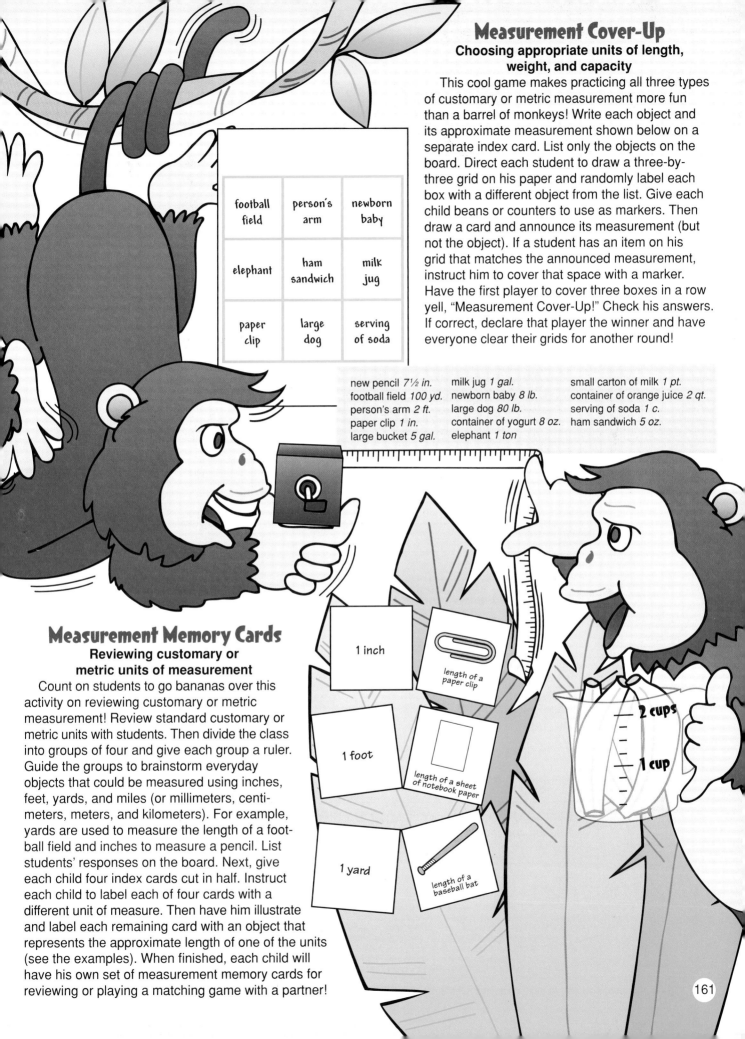

Measurement Cover-Up
Choosing appropriate units of length, weight, and capacity

This cool game makes practicing all three types of customary or metric measurement more fun than a barrel of monkeys! Write each object and its approximate measurement shown below on a separate index card. List only the objects on the board. Direct each student to draw a three-by-three grid on his paper and randomly label each box with a different object from the list. Give each child beans or counters to use as markers. Then draw a card and announce its measurement (but not the object). If a student has an item on his grid that matches the announced measurement, instruct him to cover that space with a marker. Have the first player to cover three boxes in a row yell, "Measurement Cover-Up!" Check his answers. If correct, declare that player the winner and have everyone clear their grids for another round!

football field	person's arm	newborn baby
elephant	ham sandwich	milk jug
paper clip	large dog	serving of soda

new pencil *7½ in.*
football field *100 yd.*
person's arm *2 ft.*
paper clip *1 in.*
large bucket *5 gal.*

milk jug *1 gal.*
newborn baby *8 lb.*
large dog *80 lb.*
container of yogurt *8 oz.*
elephant *1 ton*

small carton of milk *1 pt.*
container of orange juice *2 qt.*
serving of soda *1 c.*
ham sandwich *5 oz.*

Measurement Memory Cards
Reviewing customary or metric units of measurement

Count on students to go bananas over this activity on reviewing customary or metric measurement! Review standard customary or metric units with students. Then divide the class into groups of four and give each group a ruler. Guide the groups to brainstorm everyday objects that could be measured using inches, feet, yards, and miles (or millimeters, centimeters, meters, and kilometers). For example, yards are used to measure the length of a football field and inches to measure a pencil. List students' responses on the board. Next, give each child four index cards cut in half. Instruct each child to label each of four cards with a different unit of measure. Then have him illustrate and label each remaining card with an object that represents the approximate length of one of the units (see the examples). When finished, each child will have his own set of measurement memory cards for reviewing or playing a matching game with a partner!

1 inch

length of a paper clip

1 foot

length of a sheet of notebook paper

1 yard

length of a baseball bat

2 cups

1 cup

Going Bananas

Monty is going bananas over measurement! To help
him out, follow the directions below:

1. Estimate the length of each banana. Write your estimate
   in the chart.
2. Measure each banana between the bold dots to the
   nearest half inch. Record your measurement
   in the chart.
3. Answer the questions at the bottom of the page.

Banana	Estimated Length	Actual Length
1		
2		
3		
4		
5		
6		
7		
8		
9		
10		

Which unit is best for measuring each item below: inches,
feet, yards, or miles?

1. length of a tree branch _____
2. distance across the jungle _____
3. diameter of a coconut _____
4. length of a monkey's tail _____
5. height of a tree _____
6. length of a leaf _____

Bonus Box: On the back of this page, list three items that can be
measured in inches, two that can be measured in feet, and one that
can be measured in yards.

Note to the teacher: Each student will need a ruler to complete this page.

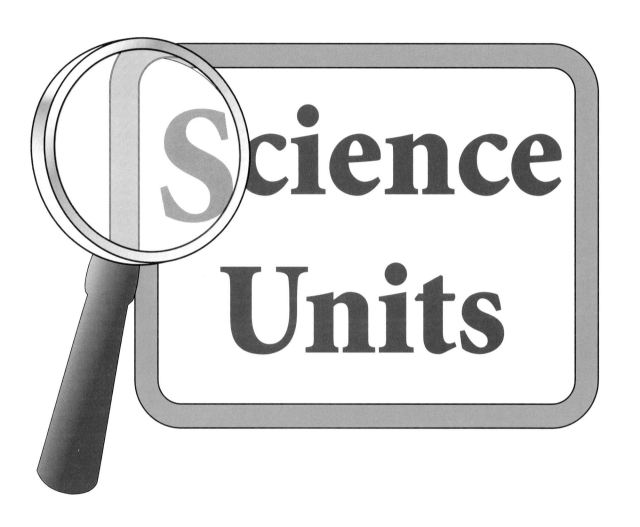

Science Units

Taking a Closer Look at Landforms

Eye Earth's ever-changing landforms with the following creative investigations!

with ideas by Liz Harrell, Highland Falls, NY

How'd We Get Those Mountains?
Folded and fault-block mountains

How are folded mountains formed? What about fault-block mountains? Have mountains of fun discovering the answers with this hands-on activity! Pair students. Give each pair two craft sticks and a small amount of clay. Then guide each duo through the directions below to help them see that a folded mountain is formed when two tectonic plates collide and force rock upward and that a fault-block mountain is formed when masses of rock move up or down along a fault.

To make a folded mountain:
1. Divide the clay in half and shape each half into flattened blocks of the same approximate size.
2. Press one side of a square onto one stick. Repeat with the remaining block of clay and craft stick.
3. Place the blocks about four inches apart on a flat surface.
4. Slide the sticks together until the blocks meet and the clay folds as shown.

To make a fault-block mountain: Repeat steps 1–3 of the directions for making a folded mountain. Then hold one stick so that its clay block remains still. Push the other block toward it until one block rises above the other as shown.

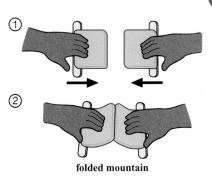

folded mountain

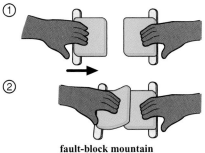

fault-block mountain

Water at Work
Water as an agent of erosion, acid rain

Nothing changes landforms like moving water! List landforms, such as the following, on the board: mountains, beaches, cliffs, canyons, deltas, valleys, lakes, and islands. Then divide students into small groups. Guide each group through the steps below to help them see water at work!

Materials for each group: copy of page 166, aluminum pie pan, damp soil, sand, gravel, small rocks, 5-oz. paper cup, pushpin, ½ c. water, pencil

Steps:
1. Shape the soil, sand, gravel, and rocks in the pie pan to form an island large enough to represent five of the landforms listed on the board.
2. Draw your island on the recording sheet. Label each landform. Then answer questions 1 and 3 on the sheet.
3. Use the pushpin to poke five small holes in the bottom of the paper cup. Hold the cup over your island and pour in half of the water. Shake the cup so that the drops rain gently on your island. Then answer question 2 on the sheet and draw how the island looks.
4. Use the pencil to enlarge the cup's holes. Hold the cup over your island and pour in the remaining water. Then answer question 4 on the sheet and draw how the island looks.

I'm Getting That Sinking Feeling!
Erosion, chemical weathering

Students have probably seen stories on TV about huge sinkholes opening up in the earth. Give your young scientists a better understanding of how something like this can happen by guiding them through the following steps to model a chemical change that can cause sinkholes.

Materials for each group: eyedropper, 5-oz. paper cup, 7 sugar cubes, ⅛ c. cookie crumbs, 2 tbsp. white vinegar

Steps:
1. Place the sugar cubes in one layer in the cup's bottom to represent underground limestone rock.
2. Pour the cookie crumbs over the sugar cubes. Press them down so that there are no holes between the sugar cubes and the crumbs form an even layer on top to represent the ground.
3. Fill the eyedropper with vinegar to represent acid rain. Hold the dropper above the cup. Squeeze the vinegar over the crumb surface. Repeat until all of the vinegar is used.
4. Observe the cookie crumb surface. *(Like limestone, the sugar cubes dissolve easily. Vinegar seeps through the crumbs, dissolving the sugar. The cookie surface collapses, creating a sinkhole.)*

The Winds of Change
Wind erosion, weathering

Expose your students to the landform-changing effects of the wind with interactive dioramas to demonstrate how sand dunes form!

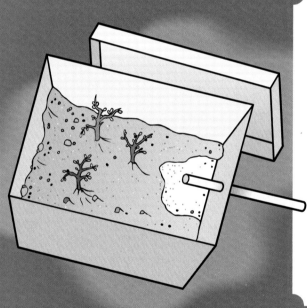

Materials for each group: shoebox with lid, clay, 3 to 5 twigs, dry soil, small rocks, sand, tape, a straw for each student

Steps:
1. Set the box's lid aside. Use a pencil to poke a hole in one end of the shoebox.
2. Push each twig into a small ball of clay. Stand the twigs on the floor of the box.
3. Place thin, even layers of soil and sand on the bottom of the box. Scatter rocks on top of the soil.
4. Place the lid on the box and tape it closed.
5. Push one end of a straw into the hole and blow once into the box. Have each group member repeat this step with her own straw.
6. Without jostling the box, remove the lid and observe the soil's surface. *(Wind can erode soil and sand, forming new landforms, such as dunes, where plants or rocks slow the wind down.)*

Chocolate Cake Mudslides
Physical weathering and erosion

Understanding mudslides is a piece of cake with this simple simulation! Bring in a 9" x 13" pan of unfrosted chocolate cake cut into squares (one square for each pair of students). Give each twosome a small cup of water and a cake square in a paper bowl. Direct one child to stand the cake square on its side and hold it, as shown, to represent the steep sides of a canyon. Have the child's partner slowly pour water on the top of the cake square until parts of it collapse and slide down. Then discuss what happened, explaining that mudslides can cause landforms to change rapidly.

Names _____ Recording sheet

Water at Work

before rain

after light rain

after heavy rain

1. What do you think will happen to the landforms after a light rain?

_____

2. What happened? _____

_____

3. What do you think will happen to the landforms after a heavy rain?

_____

4. What happened? _____

_____

The Best of The Mailbox® • Grades 4–6 • ©The Mailbox® Books • TEC61169 • Key p. 189

Note to the teacher: Use with "Water at Work" on page 164.

Friendly Forces

Electricity and Magnetism Activities

Position the magnet at one end of the nail. Slowly stroke the entire nail in one direction with one end of the magnet. Lift the magnet completely away from the nail before stroking it again.

MAGNETIC NAILS AND JINGLE BELLS
Creating a magnet

To set up this small-group center, gather a strong, medium-size bar magnet or horseshoe magnet, several medium- to large-size iron nails, small metal paper clips, and a handful of tiny jingle bells. Introduce the center by demonstrating how to magnetize a nail (see the illustration). Then post the questions shown and invite students to jingle away!

Questions:
1. Which is easier for the nail to pick up: a jingle bell or a paper clip? *(paper clip)*
2. How many strokes with the magnet does it take before the nail can pick up a jingle bell or several paper clips? *(The nail may need 40 strokes or more before it can pick up a number of paper clips or a single bell.)*
3. How many paper clips or bells can the magnetized nail pick up at a time? *(Number will vary depending on the number of times the nail is stroked with the magnet.)*

Get a charge out of electricity and magnetism with a
field of activities that's wired for success!

with ideas by Juli Engel, Midland, TX

MAKE-AND-TAKE TOYS
Assessment

To determine how much each child knows about magnetism, have him create a toy he can use to demonstrate magnetic force to younger students at your school (see the examples). Before he shares his invention, have him explain what a magnet is *(a natural or human-made object that attracts materials made of iron, nickel, cobalt, or steel)* and how his toy illustrates this force. Your eager Edisons may decide to donate the toys to their young listeners to put in a science center!

Materials: large and small baby food jars with lids, glitter, iron filings or paper clips, sand, medium-size bar magnets and horse-shoe magnets, ribbon or yarn, small objects such as the following: metallic and plastic bottle caps, screws or nuts, nails, safety pins, paper fasteners, jingle bells, pennies, marbles, confetti, tiny foil balls

Toy A: Place one to two teaspoons of iron filings or a handful of paper clips in a small baby food jar with some glitter. Screw on the lid. Tie ribbon or yarn around the lid.

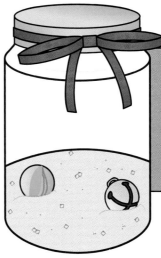

Toy B: Place a handful of sand in a large baby food jar. Add some glitter and five objects that will be attracted to a magnet and five that won't. Screw on the lid. Tie ribbon or yarn around the lid.

You and a friend are playing a board game under a tree in your backyard when you hear thunder.

FIVE-MINUTE CHARADES
Team game

For a fun way to review concepts and safety issues related to electricity, cut apart a copy of the cards on page 169. Fold the cards and place them in a container. To play, divide students into three teams. Have each team draw a card and take up to five minutes to plan how it will act out what's on the card, either demonstrating the meaning of a word or portraying a safe response to a situation. When time is up, have the teams perform one at a time. Award five points to each team giving an accurate performance. Continue in this manner until all words or situations have been acted out or you run out of time. Declare the team with the most points the winner.

Your sister asks you to plug in the iron. You notice that its cord is frayed.

TEC61169

simple
circuit

TEC61169

You are babysitting a toddler when you see her headed toward an outlet with a metal spoon in her hand.

TEC61169

series
circuit

TEC61169

parallel
circuit

TEC61169

open
circuit

TEC61169

You and a friend are playing a board game under a tree in your backyard when you hear thunder.

TEC61169

closed
circuit

TEC61169

You are washing your hands in the kitchen when your brother asks you to unplug the radio on the counter next to you.

TEC61169

Exploring Ecosystems

Eager to explore ecosystems? This collection of hands-on activities is the perfect vehicle for an exciting learning excursion!

by Dr. Barbara B. Leonard, Winston-Salem, NC

Who's Who on the Food Chain Gang?
Food chains

Time to teach about food chains? Then put this simple activity on the menu! A *food chain* is a group of living things that form a chain in which the first living thing is eaten by the second, the second is eaten by the third, and so on. A food chain always begins with plant life and ends with an animal. After explaining this information to students, discuss the definitions shown of *producers, consumers,* and *decomposers.* Then write the following food chain on the board: "seed → mouse → weasel → owl." Ask students what might happen if owls were removed. *(The weasels may increase in population and possibly run out of food.)* Weasels? *(The mice may increase in population and possibly run out of food, and the owls may decrease in population because of a lack of food.)* Mice? *(The weasels may decrease in population due to a lack of food.)* If a severe drought occurred? *(The food chain may struggle to survive if plants were in short supply.)*

Next, have each student research a food chain that consists of a producer and primary, secondary, and tertiary consumers. Afterward, give each child a black marker and four 1" x 8" paper strips in the following colors: green for the producer, orange for the primary consumer, blue for the secondary consumer, and red for the tertiary consumer. Have the student label the strips with her chain's members. Then have her staple the strips, in order, to form a chain as shown. Hang the chains from a bulletin board labeled "Meet the Food Chain Gang!"

Biological Fans
Biological hierarchy of living things

Just what is an ecosystem? The answer can be found by comparing the characteristics of an ecosystem to other levels studied in ecology. To introduce this biological hierarchy to students, list the levels shown on the board. Discuss each level, beginning with the *individual* and ending with the *biosphere.* Then have students suggest illustrations that could be drawn to represent each level.

Next, give each child colored pencils or markers and one-fourth of a cardboard pizza circle. Have the student divide the cardboard wedge into six bands as shown. Then have him label and illustrate the six levels. Encourage students to keep these easy-to-read study aids handy so they can refer to them throughout the unit.

Individual—one plant or animal that belongs to a specific species
Population—a group of plants or animals that belong to the same species
Community—many plant and animal populations living together in the same general area and depending on each other
Ecosystem—a community and its nonliving environment (soil, climate, water, air, energy, and nutrients)
Biome—many different ecosystems sharing the same geographical area and climate
Biosphere—the thin life-bearing outer layer of the earth's surface that contains all the biomes

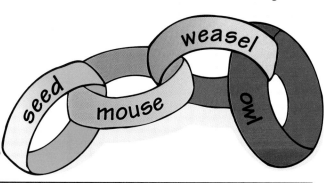

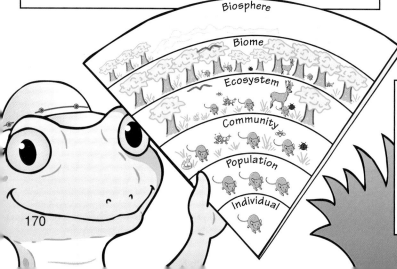

Producers—mainly green plants that use the sun's energy to produce food
Primary consumers—animals that eat plants (herbivores)
Secondary consumers—animals that eat other animals (carnivores) or both plants and animals (omnivores)
Tertiary consumers—animals that prey on secondary consumers
Decomposers—organisms such as fungi and bacteria that break down dead plant and animal material into nutrients

Making Mini Ecosystems
Creating and observing a miniature ecosystem

Want a close-up view of an ecosystem? Then make your own mini aquariums and terrariums with the simple-to-use plans listed below. Have each student make his own models, or have students help you make one of each for the class. After the models are made, instruct each child to record in a journal his observations about the animals' activities, physical changes in the bottles' environments, schedules for feeding, and schedules for changing the water in the aquarium. As you discuss students' observations, have them identify the following:

- biotic parts of each model *(the plants and animals)*
- abiotic parts of each model *(water, soil, rocks, air, sun, temperature)*
- food chain represented in each model *(aquarium—fish food → guppy, terrarium—lettuce or fruit → cricket)*
- plants' and animals' roles in the food chain *(plants—producers, animals—consumers)*
- factors to consider before more animals could be added to the models *(space, soil, air and oxygen supply, sunlight, temperature)*

After a few days of observation, release the cricket outside and send the guppy home with someone who keeps freshwater tropical fish.

Mini Aquarium

Materials: 20-oz. clear plastic bottle without cap, ruler, sand, water plant, guppy, small fish food pellets, gallon jug of water left standing for 24 hours, thermometer

Directions:
1. Cover the bottom of the bottle with a one-inch layer of sand.
2. Put the plant into the bottle.
3. Fill the bottle with water from the jug. Add the guppy and one or two fish pellets. Then insert the thermometer.
4. Each day, replace some of the water in the bottle with clean water from the jug. Keep the water temperature between 76°F and 86°F.
5. Add one or two fish pellets daily as needed.

Mini Terrarium

Materials: 2-liter plastic soda bottle with cap, scissors, ruler, soil from outside, small rocks, small plants (with roots), water, twig, cricket, lettuce leaf or slice of apple or orange

Directions:
1. Cut three inches from the bottom of the bottle. Then make six one-inch slits around the bottom edge of the top section as shown.
2. Fill the bottom of the bottle with rocks. Put one rock aside to use in Step 4.
3. Put the soil on top of the rocks. Then plant the plants in the soil.
4. Arrange the extra rock and the twig on the soil. Add a piece of lettuce or fruit.
5. Water the soil. Place the cricket inside and put the top back on the bottom.
6. Put the terrarium in a sunny spot (but not direct sunlight). Remove the top, as needed, to add food.

Can You Dig It?

How soil and water affect an ecosystem

Dig for answers about how soil and water can affect an ecosystem by having groups of students conduct this earthy experiment! Have each group follow the steps below. Afterward, have the experimenters graph the results. Then follow up with the questions below.

Materials for each group of students: six 8-oz. Styrofoam cups, sharpened pencil, paper towels, liquid measuring cup, 6 craft sticks, newspaper, trowel, 3 soil samples (1 from an area with no plants, 1 from a wooded area, 1 from a grassy area), water

Steps:

1. Make filter cups by punching holes in the bottoms of three cups with the pencil. Line the bottom of each filter cup with a small piece of a paper towel.
2. Place each soil sample on the newspaper. Observe the color and texture of each sample. Also note whether the sample contains plants whose roots are holding the soil together.
3. Fill each filter cup with a different soil sample, including any attached plants. Label the cup of soil containing no plants "A," the cup with soil from a wooded area "B," and the cup with soil from a grassy area "C."
4. Place two craft sticks slightly apart atop each remaining cup as shown. Stack a filter cup on each empty cup as shown.
5. Slowly pour eight ounces of water into cup A. When the dripping stops, remove the filter cup and craft sticks. Then measure and record the amount of water collected in the bottom cup.
6. Repeat Step 5 with cups B and C.
7. Record your conclusions about which soil retains the most water, which one allows water to pass through the fastest, and whether soils with plants hold more water than those without.

Questions:

1. Why are soil and water important to an ecosystem? (*For the most part, plants depend on soil and water to live and grow. Without plants, consumers could not live and grow.*)
2. How can soil differences affect an ecosystem? (*It is one factor that determines the type of plants and animals that can live there. Sandy soils, for example, drain faster than soils containing clay.*)
3. How does the amount of water in an area affect an ecosystem? (*All living things need water. If there is too much or too little water, plants and animals can die. Climate, topography, and soil type all affect the amount of water in an ecosystem.*)

The Build-a-Biome Game

Characteristics of biomes

Put on your hard hat—it's time to build a biome with this fun-to-play group game! Make a copy of the cards on page 173 for each group of four players. Glue each copy to a piece of tagboard. Then have the players cut out the cards and shuffle them. The object of the game is to be the first to collect all five cards for the same biome. Have students play according to these rules:

1. The dealer deals five cards to each player and places the remaining ten cards facedown in a stack.
2. The dealer draws the stack's top card and decides whether to keep it. If he doesn't want the card, he places it faceup next to the stack. If he wants the card, he takes it and discards a different card from his hand, placing it faceup next to the stack.
3. The next player to the right chooses the faceup card or draws a card from the pile and discards one from his hand.
4. Continue playing in this manner until one player has five matching cards.

To extend the activity, have students research characteristics of other biomes and make new cards to add to the game.

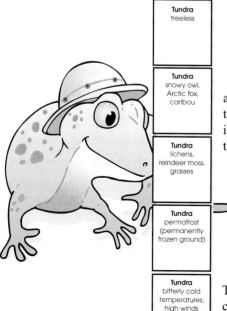

Tundra
treeless

Tundra
snowy owl,
Arctic fox,
caribou

Tundra
lichens,
reindeer moss,
grasses

Tundra
permafrost
(permanently
frozen ground)

Tundra
bitterly cold
temperatures,
high winds

Tundra treeless TEC61169	**Tundra** snowy owl, Arctic fox, caribou TEC61169	**Tundra** lichens, reindeer moss, grasses TEC61169	**Tundra** permafrost (permanently frozen ground) TEC61169	**Tundra** bitterly cold temperatures, high winds TEC61169
Temperate Deciduous Forest trees lose leaves in fall TEC61169	**Temperate Deciduous Forest** deciduous trees: oak, hickory, maple, beech TEC61169	**Temperate Deciduous Forest** deer, squirrels, foxes, birds, skunks TEC61169	**Temperate Deciduous Forest** deep, rich soil TEC61169	**Temperate Deciduous Forest** four seasons: spring, summer, fall, winter TEC61169
Tropical Rain Forest warm and moist all year with average rainfall of about 200 cm TEC61169	**Tropical Rain Forest** tree snakes, tree frogs, spider monkeys TEC61169	**Tropical Rain Forest** located near the equator TEC61169	**Tropical Rain Forest** dense canopy of vegetation, little light reaches the ground TEC61169	**Tropical Rain Forest** orchids, bromeliads, large woody vines TEC61169
Coral Reef found in warm, tropical waters TEC61169	**Coral Reef** aquatic biome made of coral TEC61169	**Coral Reef** sponges and algae grow on coral TEC61169	**Coral Reef** very old, grows slowly TEC61169	**Coral Reef** sea urchins, fishes, octopuses, snails, plankton TEC61169
Savanna tropical or subtropical grassland TEC61169	**Savanna** poor soil, few trees TEC61169	**Savanna** termites, ants TEC61169	**Savanna** animals in African savanna: elephants, zebras, giraffes, lions, rhinos, hyenas TEC61169	**Savanna** three seasons: cool and dry, hot and dry, warm and wet TEC61169
Desert *Most average less than 10 inches of rainfall per year* TEC61169	*Desert* *cacti, creosote bushes, mesquite plants* TEC61169	*Desert* *sidewinders, kangaroo rats, Gila monsters* TEC61169	*Desert* *extremes of high heat during the day and cooler temperatures at night in warm climates* TEC61169	*Desert* *dry air* TEC61169

Now Hear This!

Activities for Investigating Sound

BOTTLE BAND
Discovering how water level affects sound

Hear the sounds of familiar melodies with this "bottle-rific" activity! Round up eight identical clear glass bottles or glasses. Also gather food coloring and a metal spoon. Fill the bottles with different levels of water. Tap on the bottles with a spoon above the water line until they make a musical scale when tapped in order. Then mark the water lines on the bottles with a fine-tip permanent marker, making them easy to refill. Also add food coloring to each bottle to make the water level easier to see. Tap on one bottle at a time and have students think about how the water level affects the sound. Discuss why the bottle with the least amount of water has the highest pitch and the bottle with the most water has the lowest pitch. *(A sound is heard when the bottle vibrates. As more water is added, the bottle vibrates more slowly and produces a lower-pitched sound.)* Then number the bottles from 1 (most water) to 8 (least water) and place them at a center along with the spoon and a copy of the song sheet on page 176. Students can play Name That Tune, create their own tunes, or even blow across the bottle tops to make musical sounds!

Tune in to sound with this terrific collection of fun-to-do activities. In addition to being all ears, youngsters will be filled with good vibrations!

ideas contributed by Jennifer Otter, Oak Ridge, NC

FIRING SOUND WAVES
Observing the effects of sound waves traveling through air

Fire up students' observation skills with this flaming demonstration! Cover the end of a toilet paper tube with plastic wrap and secure it with a rubber band. Cut out a thin cardboard circle to fit the other end of the tube. Use a pencil to make a ¼-inch hole in the circle's center. Then tape the circle to the tube as shown. Next, place a small lighted candle on a table in front of the room and hold the tube so that its small hole is about one inch away from the flame. Thump the plastic with your finger and have students observe what happens. *(Tapping on the plastic makes it vibrate. The vibrating plastic makes the air in the tube travel in waves through the tube and out of the hole in the circle to the flame, causing it to flicker. If the plastic is thumped hard enough, the flame will go out.)*

To follow up, have students predict what might happen if, instead of thumping the plastic, you clap your hands together rapidly at that end of the tube. Test the predictions by having a volunteer hold the tube while you clap. Then challenge the class to brainstorm other methods of firing sound waves at the candle!

Speed of Sound Through Different Substances	
Substance	**Speed** (ft./sec.)
air	1,116
water	4,908
brick	11,980
wood (maple)	13,480
glass	14,900
aluminum	16,000
steel	17,100

Sound Conductor Clues
1. Sound travels faster through solids and liquids than it does through gases.
2. Steel and air are the fastest and slowest conductors, but not necessarily in that order.
3. The same number of substances are listed before wood as after it.
4. Water ranks between brick and air.
5. Wood conducts sound faster than brick but slower than glass and aluminum.
6. Aluminum ranks four places faster than water.

SOUND CONDUCTOR RANKINGS
Comparing the speed at which sound travels through different materials

Does sound travel better through a solid, a liquid, or a gas? Send one student at a time to this cool center to find out! Arrange the following materials at a table: glass windowpane, block of wood (maple), stainless steel cookie sheet, plastic resealable bag of water, aluminum pie tin, brick, ticking clock. Also laminate the chart and clues card on page 176; then cut them out and place them facedown on the table. Next, have a student listen to the clock's ticks traveling through the air. Then instruct her to place the clock behind the windowpane and listen to the ticking with one ear next to the glass and the other covered with her hand. Have her note on paper whether the ticking is softer or louder than it was through the air. Direct her to repeat this process with each item. Then, using the six clues for help, have her list the items in order to show how well they conduct sound. To check her answers, have her turn over the chart!

Song Sheet

Use with "Bottle Band" on page 174.

"Mary Had a Little Lamb"

4 3 2 3 4 4 4   3 3 3   4 6 6
4 3 2 3 4 4 4   4 3 3 4 3 2

"Twinkle, Twinkle, Little Star"

1 1 5 5 6 6 5   4 4 3 3 2 2 1
5 5 4 4 3 3 2   5 5 4 4 3 3 2
1 1 5 5 6 6 5   4 4 3 3 2 2 1

"London Bridge"

5 6 5 4 3 4 5   2 3 4   3 4 5
5 6 5 4 3 4 5   2 5 3 1

"For He's a Jolly Good Fellow"

1 3 3 3 2 3 4 3   3 2 2 2 1 2 3 1
1 3 3 3 2 3 4 6   6 5 5 5 4 2 1

"Row, Row, Row Your Boat"

1 1 1 2 3   3 2 3 4 5
8 8 8 5 5 5 3 3 3 1 1 1   5 4 3 2 1

"Ode to Joy"

3 3 4 5 5 4 3 2 1 1 2 3 3 2 2
3 3 4 5 5 4 3 2 1 1 2 3 2 1 1

TEC61169

Speed of Sound Chart and Sound Clues Card

Use with "Sound Conductor Rankings" on page 175.

Speed of Sound Through Different Substances	
Substance	**Speed** (ft./sec.)
air	1,116
water	4,908
brick	11,980
wood (maple)	13,480
glass	14,900
aluminum	16,000
steel	17,100

TEC61169

Sound Conductor Clues

1. Sound travels faster through solids and liquids than it does through gases.
2. Steel and air are the fastest and slowest conductors, but not necessarily in that order.
3. The same number of substances are listed before wood as after it.
4. Water ranks between brick and air.
5. Wood conducts sound faster than brick but slower than glass and aluminum.
6. Aluminum ranks four places faster than water.

TEC61169

SOCIAL STUDIES UNITS

Makes "Cents"!

The Relationship Between Taxes and Government Services

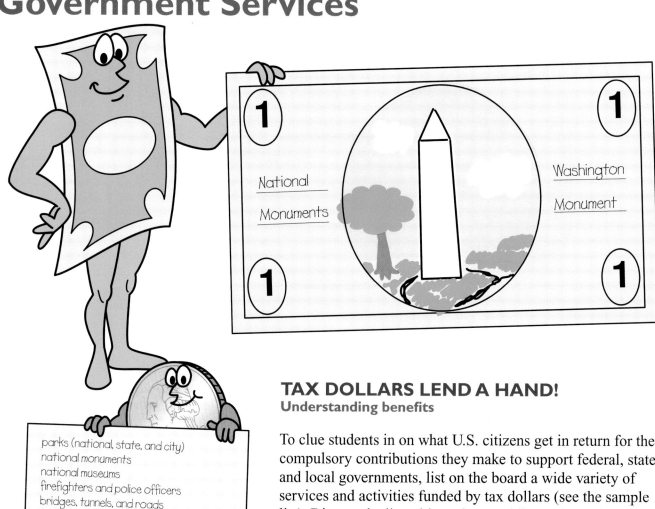

parks (national, state, and city)
national monuments
national museums
firefighters and police officers
bridges, tunnels, and roads
public schools
state universities
public libraries
space exploration
zoos (national, state, and city)
court systems (federal, state, and county)
hiking trails

TAX DOLLARS LEND A HAND!
Understanding benefits

To clue students in on what U.S. citizens get in return for the compulsory contributions they make to support federal, state, and local governments, list on the board a wide variety of services and activities funded by tax dollars (see the sample list). Discuss the list with students, adding to it any benefits the discussion triggers. Then give each child a copy of page 180 to label and illustrate as follows: on the left side, write a category from the board; on the right side, write an example of that category; and in the center, draw an illustration of the example. Display the completed bills on a board titled "Tax Dollars Make These Possible."

How are taxes and services connected? Teaching this economic concept to students is easy with these "cents-ible" activities!

with ideas by Jennifer Otter, Oak Ridge, NC

DOLLAR DECISIONS
Critical thinking, making judgments

This small-group activity gives students an idea of how tough it is for our congresspeople to choose how to spend federal tax money! Give each group a copy of a spending list such as the one shown. Briefly discuss what each category represents, giving students examples if needed. Have group members discuss the items and then rank them from 1 to 12, with 1 being the most important. Collect each group's sheet and record the rankings on a class chart. Then add the numbers together, as shown, to get a total score for each spending area. Once students order those numbers, they'll see how the class ranked the 12 areas.

Government Spending List

Spending Area	Rank (1–12)
national parks	
roads/bridges	
Medicare	
social security	
defense	
unemployment/disability programs	
disaster relief for foreign countries	
disaster relief for states	
salaries of government employees	
education	
space exploration	
environment	

Spending Area	Group Ranking	Class Total	Class Rank
national parks	3, 12, 11, 9	35	9
roads/bridges	2, 11, 6, 6	25	6
Medicare	1, 4, 5, 2	12	2
social security	5, 2, 1, 3	11	1
defense	4, 1, 3, 5	13	3
unemployment/disability programs	8, 3, 2, 1	14	4
disaster relief for foreign countries	11, 9, 8, 12	40	12
disaster relief for states	7, 8, 4, 4	23	5
salaries of government employees	12, 10, 7, 10	39	11
education	6, 5, 12, 8	31	7
space exploration	10, 7, 9, 11	37	10
environment	9, 6, 10, 7	32	8

Let's put a tax on candy and use the money to provide free dental care!

FUNNY WAYS OF FUNDING
Creative thinking

Suppose there were a tax on athletic shoes and the money from that tax would provide all Americans with free health club memberships. Such an idea is possible with this activity! Share with students that every state has a gasoline tax that is used to pay for road construction and maintenance. Explain that lawmakers felt it only fair that the people who drive gasoline-powered vehicles be the ones to pay for the roads. Next, have students brainstorm several new services they'd like the government to provide. Record each suggestion on a separate paper bag and arrange the bags in front of the room. Have each child label three paper strips—each with a different one of the services and a clever way of paying for it—and then drop the slips into the appropriate bags. When everyone is finished, read each bag's slips aloud and have the class vote on its favorite way to fund each service!

Dollar Bill Pattern

Use with "Tax Dollars Lend a Hand!" on page 178.

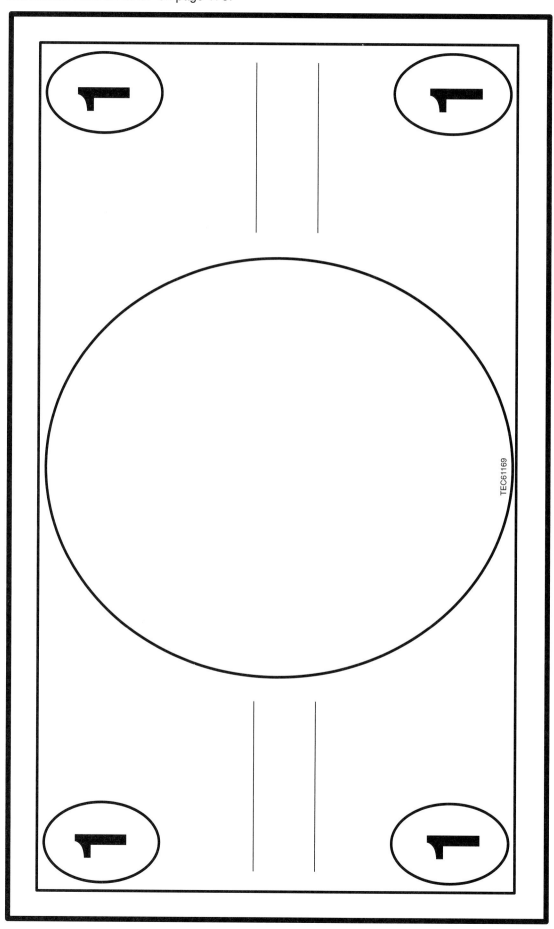

TEC61169

Decode the Taxes!

Read each clue.
Match the symbol below each answer blank to a letter in the decoder.
Then write the corresponding letter in the blank. The first one has been done for you.

1. tax on something a person buys S _ _ _ _ _

2. tax on something a person owns, such as a house or land

Decoder

A	C	E
F	H	I
L	M	N

O	P	R
S	H	T
U	X	Y

3. tax on money earned from a job _ _ _ _ _ _ _
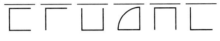

4. tax on property left when someone dies

5. tax that provides money for Americans over the age of 65

6. tax that provides money for Americans who have lost their jobs

7. tax on products imported from other countries _ _ _ _ _ _ _

8. tax on luxury items, such as furs and jewelry _ _ _ _ _ _

9. tax on property received by a friend or family member when someone dies

Bonus Box: Some states do not collect taxes on needed items such as food, clothes, and medicine. Decode the word that describes the tax status of these special goods.

Zooming In!
Focusing on a State's Physical Features

Level 1: Landforms

1. Name a landform in your state. Tell how it can be an obstacle in your game.

   Everglades National Park: Swing from vines and climb trees.

2. Tell how to get a bonus point or an extra power using the landform.

   You can get bonus points by saving endangered Everglades animals. You earn extra powers for making it past alligators.

3. Draw a picture above showing how to earn the bonus point or extra power.

VIDEO GAME VENTURE
Reviewing physical features of a state

For an adventurous review of your state's physical features, offer students the thrill of planning a video game! Have each child use a copy of the planning sheet on page 184 to design a cool video game based on three of your state's physical features: one landform, one body of water, and one natural resource. Have her complete the page as directed to decide how each selected feature could be used as an obstacle in a video game and how players could earn bonus points or extra powers. Who knows? You might see these games on store shelves one day!

Take a closer look at your state's physical features and

discover just how important they are. From landforms to bodies of water to natural resources, your shutterbugs will capture them all!

THE EFFECTS OF TIME
Critical thinking

Pretend to flip through time to document changes in your state's physical features! Discuss with students how some of your state's landforms and bodies of water could have changed since the first settlers arrived. Also discuss how the availability of natural resources could change in the future. Have each child select a landform, body of water, and natural resource from your state. Then guide students through the steps below to create a flip book that looks at physical features from a unique perspective.

Steps:
1. Stack two sheets of unlined paper on top of each other and then fold them together lengthwise to create a four-page book. Staple the pages as shown.
2. Cut two slits through the book's top three pages to create three separate sections and label them as shown.
3. Complete the "Landform" section as follows:
   Page 1: Draw a picture of your chosen landform as it might have looked to early settlers.
   Page 2: Draw a picture of how the landform looks today.
   Page 3: Draw a picture of how the landform might look in the future.
   Page 4: Write a brief summary about the land-form's changes and how the changes might affect people.
4. Repeat Step 3 to complete the "Body of Water" and "Natural Resource" sections.

MYTHOLOGICAL MARVELS
Writing a myth

Tap into your students' creativity with this writing assignment! Review with your class the different physical features of your state. Then share that some cultures often used special stories called myths to explain how such features were formed. Challenge each child to write a short myth explaining how or why either a landform, a body of water, or a natural resource in your state came to be. Once he completes his myth, have him mount his story on a colorful cutout of your state. Set aside time for each author to share his story with the class. Then post the stories on a board titled "[Name of state]'s Mythological Marvels."

183

Video Game Venture

Complete the steps for each level to plan a video game about your state.

Level 1: Landforms

1. Name a landform in your state. Tell how it can be an obstacle in your game.

   _____
   _____

2. Tell how to get a bonus point or an extra power using the landform.

   _____
   _____

3. Draw a picture above showing how to earn the bonus point or extra power.

Level 2: Bodies of Water

1. Name a body of water in your state. Explain how it can be an obstacle in your game.

   _____
   _____

2. Tell how to get a bonus point or an extra power using the body of water.

   _____
   _____

3. Draw a picture above showing how to earn the bonus point or extra power.

Level 3: Natural Resources

1. Name a natural resource in your state. Tell how it can be an obstacle in your game.

   _____
   _____

2. Tell how to get a bonus point or an extra power using the natural resource.

   _____
   _____

3. Draw a picture above showing how to earn the bonus point or extra power.

The Best of The Mailbox® • Grades 4–6 • ©The Mailbox® Books • TEC61169

Note to the teacher: Use with "Video Game Venture" on page 182.

Celebrate Citizenship!

Activities on the Rights and Responsibilities of Citizenship

Salute citizenship—with all of its rights and responsibilities—using the following creative activities and reproducibles!

with ideas by Pat Twohey, Old County Road School, Smithfield, RI

Vocabulary Explosion
Terms related to citizenship

Create a dazzling fireworks display with this star-spangled vocabulary activity! After dividing the class into pairs, give each twosome a marker and a fireworks shape cut from red, white, or blue construction paper. Assign a term listed below to each pair; then have the twosome label the cutout with its word. Next, direct the partners to research the word and write its definition on the back of the cutout. After each pair shares its term, hang the fireworks from your ceiling with string. If desired, have each student record the terms and meanings in his own word journal. Have students make their journals using these steps:

1. Place eight sheets of white paper between two sheets of construction paper (one red, one blue).
2. Staple the white paper between the covers at the top.
3. Trim the journal to make a fireworks shape as shown.
4. Write each word and its definition in the journal, one word per page. Add an illustration that symbolizes or helps explain the word.
5. Label the journal "[Your name]'s Liberty Lexicon" and decorate the cover.

We, the Citizens
Meaning of citizenship

Encourage students to reflect on what it means to be a citizen with this poetry-writing activity. In advance, collect an empty coffee can (with the lid) for each student. List these questions on the board:

- What does it mean to be a citizen?
- What rights does a citizen enjoy?
- What responsibilities or duties does a citizen have?
- Why be a member of a nation instead of acting on your own?

Divide the class into groups to discuss the questions. Then have students share their ideas as you list them on chart paper. Guide students through the list shown below, pointing out that many rights have limits. For example, the freedom of speech doesn't allow a person to harm another person's reputation by telling lies.

Next, give each student a lidded coffee can. Have each student measure and cut a piece of white construction paper to fit around the can. Have the student write a poem on the paper about what citizenship means to her. After the student illustrates the poem, have her glue the paper around the can. Challenge each group formed earlier to come up with a unique way to display the decorated cans; then vote to select the class's favorite idea. Invite other classes to view your students' salute to citizenship.

citizen

Taryn's Liberty Lexicon

Terms

alien
Bill of Rights
citizen
civil rights
Constitution
duty
freedom of assembly
freedom of religion
freedom of speech
national
nationality
naturalization
right
taxes
visa
vote

Celebrating Citizenship

by Shellie

Rights of U.S. citizens include the following:

- freedom of speech
- freedom of religion
- freedom of assembly
- right to vote
- right to run for political offices
- right to travel throughout the United States
- can't be forced to leave homeland
- can't lose citizenship except for serious actions

Unwritten Duties
Responsibilities of citizenship

Many people believe that citizens also have duties that are not demanded by the law. Challenge students to use this data collection activity to find out what others in the community think about these unwritten responsibilities. Give each student a form similar to the one shown. Instruct each child to poll a total of ten to 15 adults (family members, neighbors, and other adult friends) and fill out his form.

After students have finished their polls, divide the class into groups of four. Give each group a sheet of chart paper, a marker, and a ruler. Direct the students in each group to combine their data and create a bar graph to display their results for each question. Then instruct each group to analyze its graph and prepare an oral presentation to explain the findings. After each group gives its presentation, discuss these questions: What do the statistics tell us? How would you have answered the questions, and why?

Citizenship Poll		
Do you agree that it is a citizen's duty to...	Yes	No
Vote	₩₩₩ ₩₩₩ ₩	₩₩
Learn about public problems	₩₩₩ ₩₩₩ ₩	₩₩₩₩
Help other people in the community	₩₩₩ ₩₩₩ ₩	₩₩

Reading About Citizenship
Making connections to citizenship

Help students make connections to the topic of citizenship with the aid of some outstanding children's books. Ask your librarian to help you gather copies of the titles listed. Display the questions shown below. Then read one of the books aloud and use the questions to guide a class discussion. After the talk, divide the class into groups. Give each group one or more books, a sheet of chart paper, and a marker. Have the group list its responses to the questions on the paper. Then have groups share their responses as a class.

Books:
- *Now Let Me Fly: The Story of a Slave Family* by Dolores Johnson
- *Who Belongs Here? An American Story* by Margy Burns Knight
- *The Garden of Happiness* by Erika Tamar
- *A Very Important Day* by Maggie Rugg Herold
- *The American Wei* by Marion Hess Pomeranc
- *Granddaddy's Gift* by Margaree King Mitchell

Discussion questions:
- How is this story related to the topic of citizenship?
- What question(s) does this story raise for you?
- What is your opinion of this story?

Page 78

1. Adams, Jennifer
2. Billings, Bryan
3. Black, Sally
4. Black, Scott
5. Black, Stephanie
6. Black, Steven
7. Briggs, Melinda
8. Brown, Thomas
9. Brown, Tiffany
10. Brown, Timothy
11. Green, James
12. Green, Jessica
13. Green, Jill
14. Groth, Jonathan
15. Grove, Lisa
16. Hartman, Cassie
17. Hawkes, Paul
18. Mitchell, Kelsie
19. Simon, Kyle
20. Tyson, Sylvia
21. White, Amber
22. White, Becka
23. White, Caitlin
24. Whitman, Josh
25. Whitted, Austin
26. Young, Daniel

Bonus Box: phrase, gab, gym, gist, gnash, hors d'oeuvre, wrangle, cycle, school, tsunami

Page 79

A. Answers will vary.
B. Answers will vary.
C. Answers will vary.
Bonus Box: Answers may vary. Possible pairs include *off-on, in-out, above-below, to-from, before-after, up-down, with-without, for-against,* and *over-under.*

Page 80

1. the three friends
2. Jimmy
3. Mrs. Green
4. the three friends or the kids
5. the two treats
6. Mary
7. the clown
8. Mr. Smith
9. Mr. Moore
10. the kids

Page 81

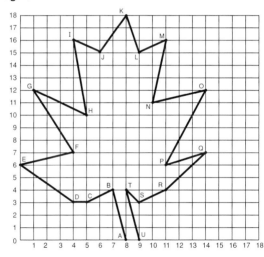

Page 82

Students' methods for solving some problems may vary.

1. 20 $(80 \times \frac{1}{2} = 40; 40 \times \frac{1}{2})$
2. 11 $(10 + 12 = 22; 22 \div 2)$
3. 1 in 23 $(1 + 2 + 3 + 4 + 6 + 7)$
4. 16 $(4 \times 3 = 12; 12 + 4)$
5. $7,225.00 ($245.00 + $1,200.00 = $1,445.00; $1,445.00 \times 5)$
6. 20 $(6 \times 30 = 180; 180 \div 9)$
7. 27 $(8 + 9 + 10 + 11 + 12 = 50; 1 + 2 + 3 + 4 + 6 + 7 = 23; 50 - 23)$
8. 168 $(8 \times 3 = 24; 24 \times 7)$
9. 6 (From 5:00 to 7:30 is $2\frac{1}{2}$ hours. From 8:30 to 12:00 is $3\frac{1}{2}$ hours; $2\frac{1}{2} + 3\frac{1}{2}$)
10. 7 $(9 + 10 = 19; 19 \div 3 = 6$ r. $1 = 7$ rounded up to the nearest whole number)
11. 16 $(10 + 11 + 12 = 33; 8 + 9 = 17; 33 - 17)$
12. $112.80 ($8.95 + $0.45 = $9.40; $9.40 \times 12)$

Bonus Box: 2 groups of drummers, 3 groups of maids (The factors of 12 are 12, 24, 36, and so on; the factors of 8 are 8, 16, 24, 32, and so on; the least common factor is 24, which is 2 groups of drummers and 3 groups of maids.)

Page 83

A. 4	E. 12	I. 10
B. 9	F. 3	J. 1
C. 11	G. 8	K. 7
D. 6	H. 5	L. 2

Bonus Box: shammes

Page 85

1. Mary baked valentine cookies, and she shared them with her friend.
2. Jason likes chocolate ice cream, but he likes strawberry even better.
3. You can address this valentine to Mark, or I can do it for you.
4. Everyone bought valentines, and we'll open them at our party after lunch.
5. I can meet you at the mall, or my dad can drive us.
6. Suzanne wants to buy the silver heart, but she doesn't have enough money.
7. Daniel thought he had set the alarm clock, but he hadn't.
8. Be sure to study your science notes, or you may not do well on the test.
9. We can have fruit punch, or we can buy soda.
10. Mike planned to be at school early, but the heavy traffic made him late.
11. Jack is playing soccer today, and we are going to see his game.
12. Jessica is bringing brownies, and Juan is bringing potato chips.

Page 86

1. $(31 - 11) - 3 = 17$
2. $3 + 14 = 17$
3. $(5 + 1) \times 2 = 12$
4. $(7 + 13) - 3 = 17$
5. $(2 \times 8) + 1 = 17$
6. $3 + 14 = 17$
7. $(100 \div 4) - 8 = 17$
8. $(30 + 4) \div 2 = 17$
9. $5 \times 3 = 15$
10. 17

Bonus Box: Problems will vary.

Page 87

1. $\frac{1}{3}$
2. $6\frac{1}{2}$
3. $3\frac{3}{4}$
4. $\frac{1}{2}$
5. $\frac{2}{9}$
6. $\frac{1}{4}$
7. $4\frac{1}{2}$
8. $5\frac{1}{4}$
9. $\frac{2}{5}$
10. $\frac{3}{4}$
11. $2\frac{3}{8}$
12. $\frac{2}{3}$

SAVE ENERGY and DON'T LITTER!

Page 88

Answers may vary. Suggested answers are listed below. The words in parentheses are the ones that are not used and should be marked out.

1. Many Americans take part in fun activities to observe Cinco de Mayo.
2. It's a time to celebrate the friendship between the people of Mexico and America.
3. We attend colorful parades and listen to speeches. (valentines)
4. Streets are decorated in red, white, and green.
5. Red, white, and green are the colors of the Mexican flag.
6. People enjoy traditional Mexican food. (bunny)
7. Some of these special foods include tortillas and guacamole.
8. Special dances and musical events are held in many American cities.
9. Famous musicians play tunes on their guitars. (sleigh)
10. Local bands play Mexican patriotic songs. (mask)
11. Dancers twirl around and snap their castanets.
12. Festivals in some cities often last for several days.
13. In Los Angeles, activities are held in the streets outside City Hall.
14. The holiday has become a celebration of Hispanic heritage. (turkey)

Bonus Box: tacos, refried beans, hot chilies, corn tortillas, enchiladas, burritos

Page 89

1. VACATION
2. BEACH
3. BARBECUE
4. BIRD-WATCHING
5. ICE CREAM
6. FIREWORKS
7. SANDCASTLE
8. BASEBALL
9. SKATEBOARD
10. CAMPING
11. BOATING
12. SEASHELLS
13. SWIMMING POOL
14. SUNTAN
15. BATHING SUIT

IT MAKES HER FEEL "DI-STING-UISHED"!

Page 90

1. $3/20$
2. $1/6$
3. $8/15$
4. $1/3$
5. $3/8$
6. $8/63$
7. $4/9$
8. $1/5$
9. $1/2$
10. $5/36$
11. $1/10$
12. $1/4$

Page 100

Answers and sentences may vary. Accept reasonable responses.

1. squeak
2. pop
3. rat-a-tat
4. zip
5. drip
6. jangle
7. hiss
8. crunch
9. tinkle
10. hum
11. swish
12. tap

Bonus Box: Paragraphs will vary.

Page 105

teacher: teacher's
teachers: teachers'
child: child's
children: children's
man: man's
men: men's
puppy: puppy's
puppies: puppies'
goose: goose's
geese: geese's
deer: deer's
deer: deer's
baby: baby's
babies: babies'

woman: woman's
women: women's
student: student's
students: students'
wolf: wolf's
wolves: wolves'
mother: mother's
mothers: mothers'
secretary: secretary's
secretaries: secretaries'
principal: principal's
principals: principals'
house: house's

houses: houses'
bus: bus's
buses: buses'
boss: boss's
bosses: bosses'
fox: fox's
foxes: foxes'
radio: radio's
radios: radios'
monkey: monkey's
monkeys: monkeys'
calf: calf's
calves: calves'

Page 108

Answers will vary. Accept all reasonable answers. Possible answers are listed below.

1. Headline: Enormous on the Loose!
   Main idea: An elephant escaped from the circus train.
2. Headline: Lion Tamer Caught in Death Grip! Main idea: Joe B. Hedded, the lion tamer, had an accident.
3. Headline: New Food Group Discovered!
   Main idea: Researchers announce that circus foods are part of a healthy diet.
4. Headline: High-Flying Wedding
   Main idea: Circus performers plan a wedding on the trapeze.

Bonus Box: Answers will vary.

Page 111

1. The <u>warm</u> <u>apple</u> pie was everyone's <u>favorite</u> dessert.
2. <u>That</u> <u>French</u> restaurant always has a <u>long</u> line of <u>hungry</u> customers.
3. He wrote a <u>popular</u> book about <u>alien</u> spaceships that invaded Earth.
4. <u>This</u> <u>homework</u> assignment took me <u>two</u> hours to complete.
5. Mom bought <u>Idaho</u> potatoes, <u>Swiss</u> cheese, and <u>Spanish</u> rice.
6. <u>Irish</u> music could be heard from inside the <u>crowded</u> <u>concert</u> hall.
7. <u>Those</u> <u>basketball</u> players can hardly fit into <u>that</u> <u>tiny</u> car.
8. We performed <u>Mexican</u> dances during the <u>spring</u> program.

Common: warm, apple, favorite, long, hungry, popular, alien, homework, two, crowded, concert, basketball, tiny, spring
Demonstrative: That, This, Those, that
Proper: French, Idaho, Swiss, Spanish, Irish, Mexican

Bonus Box: Sentences will vary.

Page 115

1. Simple Sid
2. Complex Conrad
3. Compound Carla
4. Compound Carla
5. Complex Conrad
6. Complex Conrad
7. Simple Sid
8. Compound Carla
9. Complex Conrad
10. Simple Sid

Bonus Box: Sentences will vary.

Page 119

1. These men are carved in stone // high above the fruited plain, // and visitors come to see them // from California to Maine.
2. Sweet bell of freedom, // now old and worn, // you cracked just as // our nation was born. // Years after repair, // you cracked again. // How you are now // is how you'll remain.
3. Just beside the harbor's door // stands a statue tall and sure. // She welcomes the tired, the weak, and the poor. // She lights the way to our country's shore.
4. A declaration told the king // that freedom waited in the wings. // It told him why and made it clear // that England's flag would not fly here.

1. Mount Rushmore
2. Liberty Bell
3. Statue of Liberty
4. Declaration of Independence

Bonus Box: Poems will vary.

Page 120
1. My younger brother wanted a pet. // He said he'd take anything that he could get. // But when I brought him a snake, // the kid started to quake // and fell to the ground in a sweat!
2. Consider yourself quite a fan? // Let me tell you about my neighbor, Dan. // He went opening day // and decided to stay. // Four months later, he's still in the stands!
3. Mrs. Wilson just visited Mars. // She brought us all back candy bars // that are made by wee folk // who sell eggs with six yolks // and carry their children in jars!
4. I once knew a man who had eyes // that got larger each time he told lies. // They started off small, // but in no time at all, // they'd grown to 50 times the normal size!
5. My sister plays music each spring. // She's loud and she makes my ears ring. // She's a rock and roll star, // and I'm sure she'll go far, // so long as she learns how to sing!

Page 128
Answers and reasons may vary. Possible responses are listed below.
1. autobiography and biography: Books in these two genres tell about the lives of others.
nonfiction: Factual books about the world's mountains would be classified as nonfiction.
2. fantasy: Fantasy books are about imaginary lands and may feature magical creatures.
myth: A myth features gods, goddesses, and heroes.
3. drama: A drama is a written play that is meant to be performed for an audience.
mystery: A mystery features characters who are trying to solve a crime.
legend: A legend is a story in the present or past that is based on a real event or person, such as George Washington.
4. poetry: Poetry often uses verse to express emotions and ideas.
realistic fiction: Realistic fiction features imaginary stories with believable characters and events.
5. fable: A fable teaches a moral, or lesson.
folktale: A folktale is a story that is passed on by word of mouth from one generation to another, much like what Kant's grandparents are doing.
6. science fiction: A science fiction story is based on futuristic or new scientific developments.
historical fiction: A historical fiction story is based on a real place and time in history.

Page 144
Examples of figurative language are listed in order of their appearance in the story.

the sun peeked over the horizon—personification (purple)
Andy Allen and Amy Atwater—alliteration (black)
Lucky Lure—alliteration (black)
a shiny mirror—metaphor (blue)
As quick as a wink—simile (red)
water while—alliteration (black)
rods and reels—alliteration (black)
like a rocket—simile (red)
Andy and Amy—alliteration (black)
favorite fishing—alliteration (black)
like rocks—simile (red)
in a pickle—idiom (yellow)
Where will we—alliteration (black)
Andy asked Amy—alliteration (black)
Sit tight—idiom (yellow)
trick up my sleeve—idiom (yellow)
like saucers—simile (red)

chirped cheerfully—alliteration, onomatopoeia (black and/or orange)
all around—alliteration (black)
Kerplunk—onomatopoeia (orange)
Before Andy had time to blink—hyperbole (green)
zing—onomatopoeia (orange)
He had—alliteration (black)
Lend me a hand—idiom (yellow)
fish fought—alliteration (black)
fought him tooth and nail—idiom (yellow)
sweating bullets—idiom (yellow)
stroke of luck—idiom (yellow)
lucky dog—idiom (yellow)
caught a whale of a fish—hyperbole (green)
Amy and Andy—alliteration (black)
zoomed—onomatopoeia (orange)
Lucky Lure—alliteration (black)
Wow! What a wonderful—alliteration (black)

Page 150
Colored bubbles:
6 x 9 = 54   9 x 9 = 81   4 x 6 = 24
8 x 6 = 48   12 x 12 = 144   7 x 5 = 35
3 x 9 = 27   10 x 10 = 100   4 x 5 = 20
4 x 8 = 32   4 x 9 = 36   8 x 7 = 56
5 x 8 = 40   6 x 6 = 36   9 x 7 = 63

It was <u>REALLY "FIN-TASTIC"</u>!

Bonus Box: 8 x 9 = 72, 7 x 7 = 49, 4 x 7 = 28, 8 x 8 = 64, 6 x 7 = 42, 3 x 8 = 24, 4 x 4 = 16, 0 x 8 = 0, 3 x 7 = 21, 3 x 3 = 9

Page 153
1.   2. 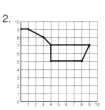   3.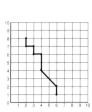
4. DRAGON
5. BIG DIPPER
6. LACERTA
Bonus Box: LIZARD

Page 156
1. $\frac{2}{9}$ 2. $\frac{3}{7}$ 3. $\frac{2}{9}$
4. $\frac{5}{8}$ 5. $\frac{2}{7}$ 6. $\frac{2}{6}$ or $\frac{1}{3}$
7. A total of seven candies should be drawn. Three of the seven should be colored purple.
8. A total of 15 candies should be drawn. Two of the 15 should be colored green.
9. A total of ten candies should be drawn. Three of the ten should be colored yellow.
10. A total of nine candies should be drawn. Seven of the nine should be colored red.

Bonus Box:
7. $\frac{4}{7}$ 8. $\frac{13}{15}$ 9. $\frac{7}{10}$ 10. $\frac{2}{9}$

Page 159
1. 78 R2   6. 97   11. 77
2. 176   7. 67 R8   12. 98 R7
3. 134 R3   8. 98 R3   13. 76 R5
4. 108 R8   9. 158 R4   14. 26 R8
5. 63 R4   10. 209 R2

No Remainder: cans 2, 6, 11
Remainder 1–3: cans 1, 3, 8, 10
Remainder 4–6: cans 5, 9, 13
Remainder 7–9: cans 4, 7, 12, 14

Page 162
Estimates for bananas 1–10 will vary.
Bananas
1—4 in.   5—½ in.   9—2½ in.
2—1 in.   6—3½ in.   10—1½ in.
3—2½ in.   7—2 in.
4—2 in.   8—1 in.

Answers may vary for problems 1–6. Possible answers are shown.
1. feet, yards   4. inches, feet
2. yards, miles   5. feet, yards
3. inches   6. inches

Bonus Box: Answers will vary.

Page 166
1. Answers will vary.
2. Gravity made the water flow downhill. As the water flowed over the soil, it eroded landform surfaces, carrying away soil particles and depositing them in other places to create new landforms.
3. Answers will vary.
4. The heavier rain caused larger amounts of soil to move downward, creating mudslides that changed the landforms.

Page 181
1. SALES
2. PROPERTY
3. INCOME
4. ESTATE
5. SOCIAL SECURITY
6. UNEMPLOYMENT
7. CUSTOMS
8. EXCISE
9. INHERITANCE
Bonus Box: EXEMPT

MAY 1 2 2011